# Full Moon Stories

## By Ann Howard

*Keep smiling!*
*Ann Howard*

# Full Moon Stories

## Author's Notes

These days it seems that many people have forgotten how to laugh. However, I am certain they are always ready for some joy—something to make them smile, grin, giggle or even laugh out loud.

People have asked why I named the book *Full Moon Stories*. Under the spell of the full moon strange and humorous things are bound to happen.

The stories in this book contain some interesting, touching, humorous and certainly memorable experiences of our family and friends. They are meant to lift your spirits and brighten your day. I sincerely hope that you enjoy reading Full Moon Stories.

Ann Howard

## Acknowledgements

My sincere thanks to those who have given me permission to share their stories. Naturally, some of the names have been changed to protect the guilty.

Many thanks also to my readers, who have given me comments and suggestions to improve and enhance this book. Those readers are, my writing companion, Margaret Amundson, Jan Needler, Penny Marx, Joy Johnston, Nancy Cairns and our three children and families, who offered comments and allowed me to use their stories. Our family: Mike and Tara Howard, Will and Kate; Tim and Lania Howard, Ella, Abby and Nate; and Beth and Jason Roach, Sam and Claire.

Special thanks to Tammie Ringas, my knowledgeable and patient friend who spent so much time helping me organize and format the book. Her encouragement and technical support contributed so much to this project. I am eternally grateful.

Finally, my heartfelt thanks to my husband Frank for supporting me in the writing of this book in countless ways: for all the carry-in meals, for his positive attitude and encouragement and for never doubting that this book would be successfully completed. My love and gratitude!

Ann Howard

Printed in the U.S.A.
Copyright 2019 by Ann Howard
Kindle Direct Publishing, 2019
ISBN: 978-1-092-10045-8

# Table of Contents

## Enough is Enough!

One rainy afternoon after going outside for the mail, I rushed back into the house and slammed my finger in the heavy front door.

"Oh, no!" I cried, thinking, *After the month I've had, I don't need this! I just hope it's not broken!*

I ran to the kitchen to run cold water on my throbbing finger. As I stood there, the telephone rang.

"Now what?" I said. The phone was within reach, and, for some reason, I answered. "Hello!"

"Good afternoon! My name is Ralph," the man said, "and I'm calling from the Mental Health Association. I'm wondering if you would care to contribute to us today."

*Swell! Another solicitor! What great timing!* "Really, I'm not interested," I said.

Nevertheless, he continued. "We give help to those with mental problems, and it would be such a help to us if you could make even a small donation."

I took a deep breath. "Look here, sir, I'm eight months pregnant, with a small child who needs lots of attention and a colicky baby who keeps me up at night. Also, I'm suffering from a miserable case of Chicken Pox, and I itch like crazy, and, with all these reds spots all over me— and I do mean ALL over—I look terrible. My husband thinks I'd be more comfortable sleeping in the guest room, but I think he can't stand to look at me. In fact, I can't stand to look at me! I caught my Chicken Pox from a friend's children, and now I've given it to my children, who are also crabby and itchy. Just last night my husband said that, these days, his favorite time of day is driving to and from work in the rush hour traffic! And, if all that isn't bad enough, I just slammed my finger in the front door and was standing here

6

running cold water on it, and praying it's not broken, when you called, asking me for money. So, give me a break! I am definitely NOT in the mood to talk to you or anyone, nor do I want to contribute to your organization today!"

"Oh, my!" he said. "You really do have some serious problems. Could I send one of our counselors to come out and help you?"

"No, oh no! But thank you, anyway. I don't need help from your organization. I'm hanging up now. Goodbye!"

Then I realized I was smiling, and, in spite of my throbbing finger, I began to giggle. My rant to the man from Mental Health must have helped me after all!

# Bosom Buddies

Angie and several friends were on a "girls' trip" to Mexico. Exhausted from sightseeing and shopping, the women decided to "call it a day." They boarded a "chicken bus" and headed back to the motel. A chicken bus is a "no frills" bus, providing an inexpensive, extremely bumpy ride from town to town, often with chickens and animals on board along with the passengers. This colorful bus had fringe strung along the front window and pictures of Jesus hanging in several areas.

The women decided that this bus could be called a "sardine bus" because the riders were packed in so tightly. There were no seats left, but there were several poles to hold onto, and the women grabbed them as the bus zig-zagged and bumped forward.

They smiled and nodded at the man and woman whose seats faced the aisle, and the couple smiled back. Suddenly, the bus lurched wildly, and Angie, losing her grip on the pole, was thrown forward. As she reached out to break her fall, much to her chagrin, she grabbed the woman's rather large breasts. Angie gasped, as did the stunned woman. The woman's husband's eyes widened and his mouth flew open.

As Angie disentangled herself and was finally able to stand upright, she said, "Oh, my! I'm so sorry! So-o-o sorry! Pardon me, please!" Immediately she realized that the man and woman did not speak English. She knew no Spanish, except for a few words and phrases like, "yes, no, how much?" and, "Where is the bathroom?" She tried to communicate her apology to the couple several more times, but was unsuccessful. Finally, she covered her face with her hands to indicate that she was embarrassed and ashamed of her clumsiness.

The man and woman, still looking dazed, did not respond, but a few moments later the woman's husband started to giggle, and then he burst out laughing. The woman, too, started to laugh. Relieved, Angie and her friends began to laugh, and soon the nearby passengers, who had witnessed the embarrassing event, joined them in the hilarity. A few moments later everyone, weak with laughter, was wiping away tears.

Later, the three friends, giggling as they discussed their recent adventure, all agreed that the incident was, indeed, a "touching" experience.

# Training Terrors

Nervous, dreading the unknown, I brought Jinks, my sweet but extremely headstrong Border Collie puppy, to our first obedience training class. Nearly a dozen equally tense owners and hyperactive puppies milled about the room. All heads turned as a stern looking woman strode into the room and glared at us.

"Heads up! Now, listen—everyone! I'm your instructor, and I cannot teach you anything until you get those animals settled down! Immediately!"

There was a shuffling of feet, and the dog owners whispered commands as they tried to get their nervous animals under control.

"Now, everyone pay attention!" The instructor paused and glared at us. Then she looked directly at Jinks, tugging at the leash, and me, struggling to control her. "I said, 'Everyone!' We have lots to do and we can't waste any time. First, I will teach your dogs to heel. Now, form a circle and walk them around the room clockwise."

As directed, tugging at the dogs' leashes, we managed to stand in a circle and began to walk around the room. Suddenly, Jinks, having none of it, slipped out of her training collar and ran about the room inappropriately sniffing other dogs, who seemed quite flattered at her attention.

Several in the class chuckled, but stopped when the instructor pointed to Jinks and screamed at me. "You—you! Get hold of that animal immediately! Get her under control!"

Her face was quite red. *Goodness, I hope she doesn't have a stroke*, I thought.

"Jinks, come!" I called out in my most assertive voice. She barely turned her head toward me, then ran away to get acquainted with the rest of her classmates. Ignoring my pleas as well as the trainer's furious commands, the pup enjoyed a lively romp around the room, stopping frequently to continue sniffing a very personal "howdy" to each dog in her path. The other owners continued to giggle at her antics, but I was certain that each one was relieved that it was not his or her wayward dog acting out and infuriating the teacher.

Three times in the first twenty minutes of class, Jinks repeated her unruly behavior, slipping out of her collar and running about the room, each time sending "Godzilla," as I had silently named the teacher by then, into a rage. By the fourth time Jinks got loose, the other dog owners, feeling sorry for me, tried to help round up my wayward pup. Unfortunately, Jinks was more agile and much faster than we were. Then suddenly she stopped, directly in front of a rather ferocious looking German Shepherd, who steadily eyed her but did not move.

"That's it!" Godzilla yelled, throwing up her hands. "That does it! Get that dog away from my dog, and bring her here, to me—right now!"

I lunged at Jinks, now standing still, obviously fascinated by the Shepherd. Fortunately, I was able to grab her and pull her to the instructor.

"Well, a major part of your problem is that collar. It's too big for your dog. And, your leash is all wrong, too," she said. "You need a leather one."

"Uh . . . sorry . . ." I said.

She frowned, then sighed loudly. "Class, wait for just a few more minutes." She glared at me. "Fortunately for you, I have a collar and leash which will fit your dog, and I suggest you buy both if you wish to remain in this class. Come over here and get them—now! Just pay me after class. We've wasted quite enough time already."

11

She put a smaller collar on the dog and handed me a leather leash. I mumbled my thanks, although I felt anything but thankful.

I wanted to run right out the door and go home, but, regrettably, I still owed the teacher money for my new equipment. Somehow, Jinks and I endured the remainder of the torturous class and Godzilla's many shouts and criticisms of the dog and me. Afterward, I paid the teacher for our equipment, and Jinks and I rushed out the door. Driving home, I said, "It's okay now, Jinks. This hell is over, and we're not coming back!"

However, at home, thinking about the situation, I realized that I owed it to Jinks and to myself to finish the class and to teach her at least the necessary commands to keep her safe. Reluctantly, we attended the rest of the classes, which were, as before, most difficult.

However, Jinks and I improved somewhat as time passed. We actually made enough progress to end the class with Jinks' receiving a conditional pass, as did every other dog in the class. The other dogs seemed much more advanced than Jinks, but apparently none of them met Godzilla's high standards for a passing certificate. Furthermore, she insisted that we all attend the next round of classes to insure all the dogs' graduation. *Hmmmm…..*

After some consideration, I decided not to repeat the class, but instead, to work with Jinks on my own, at my own pace. I suspect that most of the other owners made the same decision.

My friend Penny admitted that when her Golden Retriever Murphy went to obedience school and was trying to learn to "stay," he created quite a sensation as he repeatedly crawled on his belly from his "stay position" back to her. Where was Murphy when I needed him to take some of the attention away from my wayward pup?

Jinks, obviously quite a character with a mind of her own, surprisingly turned out to be a very good dog. Somehow, in time I managed to teach her several of the essential commands, and she and our family had a wonderful, long life together. I do not know what happened to Godzilla, but I smile as I picture her leading a unit of Green Berets into combat.

# Bravo! Bravo!

It was a beautiful Sunday morning during the Christmas season, and my daughter Beth and I were ecstatic, anticipating our family's drive into Chicago that afternoon to see The Nutcracker Suite. Even more exciting, we had second row seats, thanks to our friends Cathy and Pete, whose two children, Lauren and Kevin, were dancing in the ballet. The fact that my husband Fred and our two sons, Mike and Tim, were far from enthusiastic did nothing to darken our mood.

Fred had said, "Honey, do we really have to do this?"

"Of course we do!" I said. "Beth's learned all the music from the ballet. And the boys—even if they're not interested in going right now—will love the performance. Besides, a bit of culture won't hurt them, or any of us, for that matter! And our seats are the best in the house. It'll be wonderful, honey. You'll see!" I smiled my most encouraging smile.

"Okay, okay . . . if it's such a big deal to you girls, I guess we'll have to go. I suppose I can tape the game." He sighed, obviously martyred at giving up his Sunday afternoon football.

I chuckled, thinking of the boys' idea of entertainment—being glued to the television, eating junk food and rooting for "Da Bears!" They were certainly in for a pleasant surprise!

Finally, it was time to go. Dressed in our Sunday clothes, we headed toward Chicago. As Beth and I chatted endlessly about the ballet, Fred and the boys were unusually quiet. They were sulking now, but I knew they would catch the spirit once we were at the performance.

14

As we entered the theater, Beth beamed. She looked around. "Oh, mommy, it's so big, and so-o-o beautiful!" she said.

I nodded and glanced at Mike and Tim, who looked intentionally unimpressed by the splendor surrounding them. They plodded along as if they were on their way to the gallows, and Fred, looking martyred, walked slowly behind us.

I smiled. *They'll all be fine as soon as the curtain goes up. They'll see.*

The usher led us to our seats, and we settled in. The boys perked up a bit as the musicians began tuning up. I looked around. It was a full house. The man seated behind us had longish white hair, and he was wearing a tuxedo. I nodded and smiled at him. He stared straight ahead, as if I were invisible, his haughty look remaining unchanged. Obviously he was a ballet aficionado, and most certainly he was a snob. *No Sunday afternoon football for him!* I thought.

The lights dimmed and the orchestra began to play as the curtain went up. Grinning, Beth turned to me. This was the moment we had been waiting for! Soon we (at least Beth and I) were enchanted by the magic of it all. The scenery, the dancing, and the music were truly spectacular!

Adding a touch of elegance to the entire experience, the man behind us periodically murmured, "Bravo! Bravo!" and lightly applauded.

Suddenly the Prince, magnificent, dressed entirely in white, from his tights to his ornate jacket, danced gracefully to center stage. We looked directly up at him. He was almost close enough to touch. There was a brief hush throughout the theater. The crowd was mesmerized.

At that very moment, Beth's clear, sweet voice rang out, "Mommy, why does the Prince have that big bump right in the front of his pants?"

I gasped, and I thought I could hear the intake of breath from people sitting near us. Fred and the boys started to laugh, but stopped when I shot them a stern look. Embarrassed, Beth whimpered, covered her tearful eyes and pressed her face into my shoulder. She sniffled.

I put my arms around her, patted her and mouthed, "Shhhh." I whispered, "It's okay, honey. It's okay."

I could feel the boys shaking, then snorting as they tried, and failed, to suppress their sniggering. Fred, faking a cough and barely able to contain himself, was no help. I poked my elbow into his ribs and glared at him. He grinned at me and shrugged his shoulders. Wishing we were invisible, I sank lower in my seat. I dared not turn around.

Surely the man behind us had fainted from apoplexy by now, or perhaps he had moved elsewhere, away from the country bumpkins seated in front of him. I truly hoped that the Prince had not heard us.

Sadly, for me, the rest of the performance was a blur, a lost cause. Seeing the boys shifting in their seats, still giggling, fighting the urge to laugh and occasionally snorting, I feared they would lose complete control and that Beth would start crying again.

Sitting very still with a smirk on his face, Fred gave me a periodic nudge in the ribs. I gave all three "boys" my best "teacher look" and shook a warning finger at them. Then I prayed hard for their silence and tried to ignore them.

Time dragged on, and my prayer was finally answered as the curtain fell. Later I thought about what an unexpected and unforgettable "performance" we had provided for those around us. I had to smile as I remembered, too, that we had heard nothing from the man behind us after Beth's innocent, but audible question. He had not clapped or said, "Bravo! Bravo!" again.

One thing is certain: Our family, among others, will always remember that performance of the Nutcracker Suite.

## Meeting the Folks

Going to the dentist tops my list of least favorite things. After ignoring discomfort in several teeth for as long as I dared, I made an appointment with my dentist. He examined me, then gave me a concerned look. I sighed, awaiting the bad news.

"Unfortunately, several of your old fillings have deteriorated, and they're irritated—and possibly infected. We need to replace them as soon as possible," he said.

The dreaded day arrived much too quickly. I trudged into his office and settled uncomfortably into his padded chair.

"This will take a while," he said. "Since the deeper filling is in the left upper jaw and there's another in the lower left jaw, I'm going to give you two shots in the left upper gum, one in the lower one and another in the right side, where there's a small filling that's also gone bad. The shots will prevent your having any pain."

I shivered. "O-okay."

"Trust me, you won't feel a thing." He smiled.

*Oh, yeah, I bet I won't!* I thought.

"Believe me, you'll be fine," he said, as he gave me the first shot.

I winced. "Oooh!"

He patted my shoulder. "Well, the shots aren't fun, but the pain lasts only a few seconds, and after that, you won't feel anything else."

When he gave me the next two shots, I managed not to gasp. Soon, as promised, I felt no more pain. In fact, I had no feeling at all on both sides of my face.

After working for what seemed like quite a while, he stepped back, smiled and said, "All done! For a time you'll feel nothing, and then a bit of discomfort, but only for a short time." He smiled. "Soon you'll be good as new."

"Well, shank you," I said. We both laughed.

"That side of your mouth and your face will stay numb for a few hours, and then you'll be back to normal."

I smiled what felt like a lopsided smile. "Thatsh good!"

After I left his office, I stopped at a nearby grocery store to get a few things for dinner. As I rounded the first corner, I practically bumped into the parents of my daughter Beth's boyfriend, Ken.

"Well, Her-row!" I said and smiled my lopsided smile.

Looking stunned, and rather uncomfortable, they mumbled a greeting.

*Oh, no!* I could feel my face getting hot. *They probably think I'm crazy, or drunk! I'd better explain.*

"I jusht finischt a dentish appointmentsh and sho my fashe ish all froshen becaush itsch shtil numb."

"Wh-What?" Ken's mother said. His father simply stared at me.

I explained again, more slowly. "My fashe . . . ish . . . shtill numb . . . from a dentish . . . appointmentsch."

"Oh, uh . . ." his mother said, looking most uncomfortable. "Well . . . it was . . . nice . . . seeing you."

"Sho nishe to she you, too. G'bye!" I said, attempting to smile again.

Without another word, they scurried away and quickly ducked around the corner to the next aisle.

"Well, I shirtenly meshed that up!" I mumbled.

I rushed to the checkout counter, paid, picked up my sack of groceries and hurried to my car. Humiliated, I drove home. However, as I thought about the incident, I began to smile. It really was funny—almost like a slapstick comedy. I chuckled.

By the time Beth came home from school, my numbness had almost worn off. Laughing, I described the comical encounter with Ken's parents to her.

"Oh, mo-ther! I don't think it's a bit funny. It's just . . . terrible! What will they think of us?"

Horrified, she turned away and stomped off toward her room.

I called to her. "Sorry, honey! Sorry! Do you want me to call them and explain?"

"No! O-o-oh, no! You've done e-nough!"

I giggled. *Ah, teenagers!* I knew she would get over it. She would explain what had happened to Ken, and eventually she would be able to laugh about the incident. And, soon after, she was able to see the humor of the situation.

Furthermore, she had to admit that I had made an unforgettable impression on Ken's parents!

# On the Trail

The present day turbulent political climate brought to mind several incidents that happened during a political campaign some years ago. After my good friend Janet Moran and I had co-chaired a neighborhood group which, against the odds, succeeded in getting a much needed levee on the Little Calumet River, our neighbors urged us to run for two open City Council seats. I quickly declined, but Janet said she would run only if I would be her campaign chairman. After much consideration, I agreed.

We faced a formidable challenge. No one from our political party, and certainly no women, had been elected to a Council seat in our city for 28 years. Furthermore, her opponent was the city's Officer Friendly, a popular policeman from a respected family that had run a successful local business for many years. We joked that running against Officer Friendly was like running against the Easter Bunny and Santa all rolled into one.

Knowing that contacting the 15,000 registered voters in our district and plunging headlong into the murky world of politics would be a formidable task, we two naïve, inexperienced housewives hit the campaign trail. Day after day, we rose early, made breakfast, packed our children's lunches and drove them to school. Then we rushed home, donned our tailored, neutrally colored "campaign" dresses and marched out to knock on doors and spread the "good word."

Although we met some very nice people, we also encountered barking dogs, strange characters and some people who were obviously bored, and even barely tolerant of us. Not once, but several times, people saw our campaign buttons and, without a word, slammed their doors shut.

One man did take the time to yell, "A woman's place is in the home!" before slamming his door.

A disapproving woman shook her finger at Janet and said, "You should be at home fixing your husband's dinner."

Janet smiled and said, "It's at home in the crockpot." The woman scowled and shut the door. We shrugged, knowing, "You can't win 'em all!"

Fortunately, there were also friendly, encouraging people on the trail. One woman refused to listen to our platform, but promised to vote for Janet simply because Janet was a woman. Of course, we were happy for her vote, but frustrated to be unable to deliver our sincere, well thought-out message.

After hours of campaigning, we would rush back to school to pick up our carpools, prepare dinner and help the children with homework before putting them to bed. Some evenings we would go out again to attend political meetings or rallies. Most nights, exhausted, we would crawl into our beds. Day after day we repeated the routine. We were determined. No matter how tired we were, we persisted.

We threw a fundraiser in order to buy political signs for Janet. Then we asked people to display the signs in their windows or yards. One woman was clearly undecided.

"Well . . . I . . . really don't know. I'm not even sure where I'd put one."

Janet was not taking "no" for an answer. "Well," she said, rather assertively, "you just step outside, and I'll tell you just where you can stick it."

I gasped. Janet's face turned crimson as she clapped her hand over her mouth. Looking stunned, the woman opened her mouth, but did not speak.

After an awkward pause, suddenly all three of us exploded into laughter.

Janet stammered an apology, and I managed to regain control long enough to say, "Now I know why campaign managers keep a close watch on their candidates. You never know what will come out of their mouths!"

My remark set us all off again. After we recovered from our hysterics, the woman agreed to post Janet's sign. Victorious, we went on our way, still chuckling. We knew that this was a voter who would surely remember us.

We knocked on one door several times and were about to leave when a man, wrapped only in a bath towel, suddenly opened the door.

"Yes?" he said, while struggling to hold back his barking dog. His towel began to slip, and he grabbed at it with his free hand.

Determined not to stare, Janet said, "Uh . . . I'm Janet Moran, and . . . I'm running for City Council in this district. I-I would like to talk to you . . . but . . . well, why don't I just give you this brochure explaining my reasons for running?"

Looking most uncomfortable, shifting from one foot to the other, he said, "Well . . . um . . ."

Now we were in a fix. The man, holding his towel and his dog, had his hands full. *What could we do with the brochure?* He had no mailbox, nor an obvious place where we could put it.

"Sooo . . . I'll just leave it . . . here . . . at the door," Janet said, and laid it on the porch floor.

He simply shrugged, and we turned and hurried away, trying not to watch him attempt to close the door. With some difficulty, we managed to suppress our laughter until we were out of earshot.

When we stopped laughing, I said, "Well, it could be worse. At least you didn't offer him a sign and tell him to step outside so you could tell him just where to stick it!"

This was yet another voter who would not forget us! Nor did we forget him or other humorous incidents on the campaign trail. We laughed about them many times during those hectic months, which, after visiting every household in the district, finally culminated with Janet's incredible win.

Careful to guard her words during her subsequent campaigns, Janet easily won her seat on the City Council twice more before retiring.

# A Lunch Break

Mary, my sister-in-law, and her husband Bill owned a very lively, curious and extremely smart Jack Russell Terrier named Becca. As was their custom, one day Bill and Becca were taking a walk along the golf course behind their home. Bill unleashed Becca for a brief run, and she scurried ahead, then disappeared around a bend. He hurried to follow her.

In a short while he spotted the dog alongside two workmen who were bent over with laughter. Bill called to Becca, and she wagged her tail and ran toward him.

"Is this your dog?" one of the men asked. He was grinning and wiping away his tears.

Bill said, "Yes, she's my dog Becca."

Among bursts of laughter, the man related this story. "My buddy and I left the truck to pick up some branches that had blown down. This little mutt ran toward us and wagged her tail." He stopped to chuckle. "At the very last second she turned toward our truck and jumped up, clear through the window, and into the truck. We couldn't believe such a little runt could jump so high!"

"I can't either," said Bill, shaking his head.

"Well, by the time we walked back to the truck," the man said, "she had eaten both of our sandwiches—pulled them right out of the sacks and ate them! Only the bags were left." He grinned. "Obviously, she has good taste. She doesn't like plastic!"

All three men laughed, and Becca, enjoying the fun, wagged her tail.

"Well . . . I'm really sorry," said Bill. "Can I buy you two some lunch? It's the least I can do."

The man said, "No, but thanks, anyway. It won't hurt either of us to miss a lunch now and then. Besides, it was worth losing our lunches just to see what this amazing acrobatic dog could do. Man, she could join the circus!"

*That, she could*! Bill thought, smiling, as he walked Becca home after her lunch break. *One thing's for sure! Becca is one dog who never lets her size get in the way of her desires!*

# Love Is Blind

Doris beamed. Today, August 19, 1967, had been the most exciting day of her life—her wedding day! It had been even more beautiful, more magical, than she'd ever imagined. All dressed in pristine white, she was the picture-perfect bride.

A good Catholic girl, Doris had heeded the admonitions of her mother and, of course, the nuns at school. She could still see Sister Serena shaking her finger at the young girls in her class, admonishing them about the evils of sin and lust. And Doris had heeded their advice, always taking the high road. Even when pressured by those eager high school boys, and, later, by several ardent and charming college men, she had resisted.

But this was her night, the night for which she had saved herself. Checking her appearance one last time in the bathroom mirror, she smiled. Her flowing soft white negligee made her feel like a princess, and, thank goodness, her hairdo had survived the long day and evening.

Oh, how she had worried about her hair and what a sight she would be tomorrow morning! A restless sleeper, she often awakened with wild, scarecrow hair—not the best look for a new bride. Fortunately, she had found the ideal solution in a magazine ad. The Magic Turban, a soft, scarf-like hat, was guaranteed to keep even the most wayward tendrils in check. She put on the turban, looked in the mirror and turned her head slowly to each side. The turban added a rather elegant touch to her ensemble. *Yes, it was perfect!* She smiled and walked slowly to the door. She was deeply in love, and she was ready.

She opened the bedroom door, and Randy, more handsome than ever, walked toward her with outstretched arms. They met, they kissed, and she forgot all else except how ecstatic she was in the strong arms of her husband. Randy picked her up and carried her to the bed, where he gently laid her down, then joined her. He reached over and turned the light down to a soft, romantic glow. Breathless, she closed her eyes.

*Oh, my*! she thought, surrendering to the dizzying passions of their long-anticipated wedding night. *Oh, my. . .*

In the midst of their caresses, she opened her eyes to gaze at her Prince Charming. She blinked, then gasped as she stared into utter blackness.

She shrieked, "Oh, Randy! Oh, my God, Randy!"

"Doris, what's wrong?"

"Oh, Randy, I can't see! I'm . . . I'm blind! I'm blind!"

"What? You're blind?"

"My mother warned me about this. She said if I went too far, something terrible would happen to me—that I'd become terribly ill, or I'd go blind! And I have! I've gone too far, and I'm being punished! I've gone blind! Oh, God, help me!" She began to cry.

For a moment she heard nothing. Then she heard Randy's gasp and strange, muffled sounds. *Was Randy crying, too? How sensitive of him!*

"Oh. . . D-Doris, Doris. . ." he said.

Again she heard those sounds, almost as if he were hiccoughing, or choking. Then Randy's hand brushed her face, and suddenly, there was his face, his beautiful face! And he was wiping away his tears. *How sweet!*

She thought, *Those are definitely tears, but . . . Randy isn't crying. He's . . . laughing? Laughing at a time like this? How could he?*

"Oh, sweetie," he said, "You didn't go blind." He put his hand over his mouth to suppress another giggle. "It . . . it was your Magic Turban. It slipped down, over your eyes!"

"Wh-what?" Doris felt her face go warm. *How ridiculous!* She started to giggle, and then she laughed.

She and Randy completely lost control, laughing until they were weak, wiping away their tears and holding their aching sides.

Finally Doris was able to speak. "Well, Randy, I guess what they say is true—love IS blind after all!"

## Really True Grit

After an endless night with Tim, our fretful baby, Monday morning came much too early. Moving in slow motion to ease the throbbing in my head, I tiptoed past the nursery and down the stairs. The baby, who was teething, had fussed for hours before falling asleep. Mercifully, Mike, our two-year-old, had slept through the night's turmoil and was still asleep.

As I reached the bottom step, the phone rang, shattering the silence.

"Oh, no!" I muttered, stumbling over a toy truck in my haste to answer it. Too late! The little guy began to cry.

"Hello," I said.

"Ann, dear . . . it's . . . mom . . . tell you . . . bad news." I strained to hear, as my mother-in-law's voice crackled over the bad connection.

"What, Mom?" I whispered. "Bad news?" I could not hear her as the static and the baby's fussing became louder.

"Sorry, Mom! I can't hear you," I said. "I'll have to call you right back . . . Mom? Mom? Did you hear me?"

No answer. We had been disconnected.

I rushed upstairs and scooped up Tim in my arms. "Sh-h-h, sweetheart. It's okay now. Mommy's here with you. Sh-h-h," I crooned and began to rock him back and forth.

His eyelids fluttered and his eyes closed as he began to relax. I continued to rock him gently until he drifted off. I tiptoed downstairs, laid him beside me on the couch and dialed the phone.

"Hello?" Mom said.

"Hi, Mom. The connection's better. I can hear you now. What's going on?"

"Oh, my, I have terrible news! You know Mrs. Curtis, Aunt Rose's mother? She's passed away."

"Oh, I'm so sorry. She was very sweet."

"Yes, yes she was."

Tim began to fuss again.

"Hush now," I said.

"What?"

"Oh, no, not you, Mom. I'm trying to calm the baby down. Please go on." I stroked Tim's forehead, picked him up with one arm and began rocking him again.

"Well," she said, "The memorial service is this coming Wednesday."

Tim yawned, and his eyes opened, then closed. *Thank goodness!* I thought

"This Wednesday? That soon? Today's Monday. Should we send flowers, or do you think Aunt Rose would prefer a donation of some kind?"

"Well, she's so distraught now, over the shock of it all. Mrs. Curtis wasn't even sick. There are so few left in her family, and those folks are fairly old. We're really her family now, and we need to support her."

"Of course," I said.

"And . . . I was thinking, just thinking, mind you, that since you and Fred are the only ones who live near her, in the same town, perhaps you might be willing to have a little family dinner, something simple, after the service. That would be such a lovely thing to do."

"Oh, well . . . I . . ."

"Of course," she said, "we could always . . . have something at a restaurant, but . . ." Then her voice trailed off.

"Well, that just seems so . . . cold."

I looked around the house. "Uh, well I . . . guess . . . I might . . ."

*What am I thinking? I have a teething baby and a toddler, and this house is a mess with toys, last night's pots and pans, Fred's papers everywhere! Am I crazy?*

"Oh, dear, that would be wonderful! I knew you wouldn't let me down!"

*Did I say I could do it? Did I, really? I didn't think I did! I have such a big mouth!*

"Well . . . how many people would you guess there'd be, Mom?"

"Oh, I'd say probably no more than ten, but possibly up to . . . maybe eighteen or twenty."

I swallowed hard. "I have only eight dining room chairs, and it might be a bit crowded."

"Oh, surely your neighbors have a few you can borrow. Maybe you could cook one of those delicious roasts you make. The family loves your roast, and maybe a cake. Your German chocolate cake is delightful. Let's see, now . . . we'll need potatoes and a vegetable, too. I can bring a salad and some rolls, and flowers from my garden. I'll get the details about the service and a head count, and then I'll get back to you as soon as I can."

"Thanks, Mom." *Thanks? Am I nuts? Thanks?*

"And don't even think of sending a donation or flowers. What you're doing is so much better. Well, I'd better start making some calls. I'll get back to you. You are an angel! Bye now, dear!"

"Bye, Mom." *Good grief! What have I gotten myself into?*

I looked around. The house looked as if it had been ransacked, and the scent of ammonia wafted from the diaper pail. *What's wrong with me? I have no time, not even three days to—to perform a miracle! Well, really, how bad can it be? I have only a few small chores, like tending to the kids,*

32

*shopping, cleaning house and preparing a meal for ten, maybe twenty people! Piece of cake! Oh, yes, and we need a cake, too! But wait! There's a bright spot. I won't have to make a salad or rolls or even get a flower arrangement for the table. Happy day!* I tiptoed upstairs, tucked the baby into his crib, then sat down and cried.

After the boys awakened, I dressed and fed them, packed them into the station wagon and set off for the grocery store. After a challenging forty minutes there with the two boys, I came home and unloaded the car, fed the boys lunch, played with them for a bit and put them down for a nap. During my "golden time," I took a stab at "stashing and stowing," my form of speed cleaning, and decided it was grilled cheese or nothing for dinner.

After dinner, Fred rushed off to teach a night class at the local college, and the boys had a short play time before baths and bedtime. Then I sat down to make a to-do list for Tuesday and promptly nodded off. When Fred came home, I rallied briefly, then stumbled off to bed.

After another night punctuated with bouts of Tim's fussing, it was suddenly Tuesday—with only one day left! I sandwiched in a bit more cleaning to the cacophony of the boys happily banging on my pots and pans. About midday my mother-in-law called to say that definitely twelve, possibly fifteen would be coming to dinner after the service. The boys and I dashed off to the store to buy another roast, and I called a neighbor to ask if I could borrow some chairs.

During naptime, I turned on the oven and whipped up a box German Chocolate cake, praying that no one would notice that it wasn't homemade. As I opened the oven door, I gasped. The oven was stone cold! I felt stone cold, too. *Now what?* I called Karen, my good friend and neighbor, and explained my predicament.

"I'll turn on my oven and then I'll be right over to get the cake. Make a list of anything else I can do to help."

"Thank you! You're truly a saint!" I said.

It was too late in the day to get the oven fixed, but I knew that Fred, my brilliant engineer, could fix anything. That evening he probed, tested and tinkered with the stove, frequently verbally abusing it. Thank goodness, the boys were in bed!

Finally, he threw up his hands. "It's shot! The oven's dead! That thing was ancient when we bought the house. We'll just have to replace it."

"It—it can't be dead! Can't you revive it? We have all those people coming for dinner tomorrow. I have to cook a roast, potatoes and a vegetable casserole. What can we do now?" Tears cascaded down my cheeks.

Fred thought for a few minutes. "Calm down. We can do this. I'll bet Karen will help us. You can make everything ahead and take it to her. Then she can cook it and keep it warm while we're at the service. We can bring it back here on our way home."

Karen readily agreed. "Make me a schedule of cooking times, and we'll be all set."

We fed the kids, put them to bed and ordered a pizza, then spent the evening cleaning the house.

Finally Fred said, "The house looks good, but I'm just too tired to push that big stove back tonight. I'll do it in the morning before we leave. That thing obviously hasn't been moved in years. While it's away from the wall, why don't you clean that dirty floor under it? "

"Okay. Not tonight, though. I'll do it in the morning," I said, and we trudged upstairs and fell into bed.

Several hours later Tim began to fuss. "Blasted teeth!" I said as I began the nightly pacing and cuddling

34

ritual. Mercifully, in half an hour he settled down and fell asleep. Even he could not stay awake three nights in a row!

Early Wednesday, promising to be home in several hours, Fred left the house to hastily tidy up several projects at work. I tiptoed downstairs to get a head start on preparations before the boys awakened. I glared at the stove. It looked dead, cold and white. Hard as I scrubbed, my soap would not clean the floor, sticky with years of accumulated grease and grime. Finally, my trusty Comet Cleaner did the trick.

When the boys awakened I fed them, then gave them several of my pots and pans, now their favorite toys, while I began making the vegetable casserole.

Karen appeared at the door. "I'm here to help. What can I do?"

"Sit down and have some coffee. You're doing enough—more than enough," I said. "Thank you again for saving the day! I'll have this vegetable casserole done in a few minutes, and then you can take it back with the rest."

I finished chopping the onions and began layering them with the other vegetables and seasonings.

"That looks good," she said.

"It's Fred's aunt's recipe, and it's one of my favorites. I just have to add the finishing touch, the Parmesan cheese." I shook the can, then generously sprinkled the cheese on top.

"Oh, no! Stop!" she said, pointing at the casserole.

I looked down at the light green powder covering the top of the casserole. It certainly was not Parmesan cheese! The cheese was still on the counter, and the shiny green can in my hand was Comet Cleaner!

"No way!" I said, shaking my head. "Those are all the vegetables I have!"

"Well, forget that dish! You can't save it now," she said.

I stood there for a few seconds, then smiled. "Oh, yes, I can. I can fix it!"

Taking my largest spoon, I dug deep, scooping off the layer of powder, which I threw into the garbage.

"Tell me you're not going to serve that. You're not, are you?" she said.

I smiled as I sprinkled a generous layer of Parmesan cheese over the top. "There! It's good as new!"

"You're really going to serve it?"

"Really! I am. I'm desperate. Besides, I scooped off all the Comet Cleaner. It'll be fine. I'm sure . . . well, pretty sure!"

She shook her head. "You're unbelievable!"

I grinned. "It's our little secret. And really, a little grit might be good for the digestion. We probably swallow a lot worse than this in a day's time."

We were still laughing as we loaded the food into her car. "See you later, crazy lady!" she called out as she drove away.

I tidied the kitchen and dressed the boys just before Fred came home. We pushed the stove back in place and drove off to the memorial service. Afterward, we rushed out of the church and stopped at Karen's to load the steaming food into our trunk. We arrived at home minutes before the guests.

A short while later we sat down to a lovely meal of roast beef, potatoes, Mom's salad and rolls and a delicious vegetable casserole, followed by chocolate cake and ice cream. Everyone enjoyed the meal.

Later, after the guests had left, Karen called to see how the dinner had gone.

"Thanks to you, my friend, it was perfect! You really saved the day!" I said.

"And, how did they like your very interesting vegetable casserole?"

"They loved it! Several even asked for the recipe. And, guess what else? Never did I see such big smiles and such pearly white teeth!"

"You really are crazy!" she said, and we shared a hearty laugh.

# Anniedotes

## Ball Game

"Want to play ball?" said Lincoln.

"Sure," said Grandma Jill.

"Okay, you be the batter, and I'll be the mitter!"

. . . . . . . . . .

## Pretty Baby!

One day three-year-old Stella was playing with her dolls. Her father walked up to her and picked up a doll.

"Oh, look at me! I'm just s-o-o-o pretty!" he said in a falsetto voice as he twirled the doll and pranced from side to side.

With a sober face, Stella shook her head, paused for a moment, then looked at her mother. She shrugged her shoulders and rolled her eyes. "You gotta love 'em, don't ya?" she said.

. . . . . . . . . .

## The Mouths of Babes

Three year-old Doug had locked himself in the bathroom, and, frantic, he sobbed uncontrollably.

His mother, standing outside the door, said, "Douggie, you have to calm down. You'll be okay, I promise. I'm going to go call the Fire Department now, and soon a fireman will come and help me unlock the door so you can come out. Okay?"

"Mom-my, I'm so sc-scared! I'm all alone!" he cried.

"Now, honey, you are not alone. Remember, God is there with you. He's always there to protect you and to watch over you. I'm going to go call the fireman now, and then I'll be right back. Okay?"

"O-okay, Mommy, but h-hurry back!" he said.

"I will, honey," his mother said as she raced away to telephone the Fire Department. A man answered her call immediately, but he told her to wait for another person to come to talk to her. She waited impatiently for a few minutes, and then another man answered and assured her that a fireman was already on the way.

She rushed back to the bathroom door. "Doug?" she said softly. There was no answer. She wondered if he had cried himself to sleep. "Douggie?"

Then she heard Doug's small voice. Whispering, he said, "Is . . . is that you, God?"

. . . . . . . . . .

### E-mail from our son Tim, regarding injuries and ailments of children, Ella, Abby and Nate

Hi, Mom and Dad,

Well, we set a record with six doctor's visits this week! One fishing weight to the eye, one scooter accident and four confirmed cases of Strep Throat. We still managed to take a nice hike and run a 10-miler this weekend. All are healed and feeling better now.

. . . . . . . . . . .

### E-mail from son-in-law Jason
### (To our daughter Beth, away on a business trip)

Hi, Mommy,

Claire insisted on wearing a very formal big fluffy pink dress today to school, and I didn't have time to protest, so she's kind of got a "prom queen" look going. Sam's fly on his jeans wouldn't zip, but I'm hoping no one will notice. All I had left for lunch bread was heels, so I cut them up funny and told the kids they were getting "crazy triangle sandwiches" today. Then I realized I had let our neighbor Michele borrow our car seats, so we rode "big kid style" to school.

Come home, Mommy!

. . . . . . . . . .

### Story from a nurse friend

Mrs. Smith brought little Jimmy to the doctor's office and said, "Could you please check his throat? It's full of 'muck-us.' "

It took all of the nurse's restraint to keep from laughing. Stepping into the doctor's office, she said, "Mrs. Smith and Jimmy are here. She wants you to check his throat because it's full of—she raised her eyebrow—'muck-us.' "

The doctor grinned. "Send her in."

After the examination, the Smiths left the office. The nurse said to the doctor, "Well, did little Jimmy have 'muck-us' in his throat?"

"No," said the doctor. "Actually, it was peusse!"

. . . . . . . . . .

**(Said by an impatient woman standing in a very long line at Disney World)**
"You'd think people would know better than to bring children to a place like this!"

. . . . . . . . . . . . . . . . . . . . . . . . . . . . . . . . . . . .

# Such a Deal!

"Here's to Disney World! Such a deal!" Teresa and C.J. poured two glasses of wine and toasted their upcoming family trip. It was the trip of a lifetime—a bargain package including air fares, hotel, admissions and even transportation to and from the Park. It was spring break for the kids, and C.J. had taken the time off from work. Even more exciting was that their son Gus' birthday was on the last day of the trip. This was a birthday the entire family would remember!

The boys—Gus, four, Leo, seven, and Drew, ten— were the perfect ages to appreciate the rides, the shows and the entire Disney extravaganza. Teresa had researched every Disney offering she could find and had selected various age-appropriate adventures for the family. As she completed the day-by-day itinerary, she was confident that it included something for everybody, and even the grownups. The entire family was giddy with anticipation!

All was ready. The boys were in bed, and the suitcases and duffel bags, stuffed with snacks and books for the boys, sat at the front door. Knowing their adventure would begin quite early in the morning, Teresa insisted that everyone go to bed early in the evening.

Their flight was right on schedule, and they were excited to find that their hotel was directly across the street from Downtown Disney. Their room was also a pleasant surprise—a tastefully decorated two-bedroom suite with three baths and a kitchen with a refrigerator and microwave. After they checked in and unpacked, they spent the remainder of the day relaxing and enjoying the pool and the many accommodations of the hotel. Elated, but exhausted, they went to bed early to be ready for their first day at the Magic Kingdom.

In the morning they rushed to the shuttle and, once aboard, headed for the Teacup ride. A few minutes into the ride Gus said, "Oh, my stomach! It really hurts—bad! I think I'm gonna throw up!"

"Oh, no! Can you make it back to the room?" Teresa said.

Gus nodded. "I-I think so . . ."

As soon as the ride was over, Teresa said, "C.J., you take Leo and Drew on the next ride. Gus and I'll catch the shuttle back to the hotel."

"I can go with Gus," C.J. said.

"No, you stay with the boys. I don't want to spoil their first day. I'm sure Gus will feel better soon. I'll let him rest a while and meet you in a few hours."

C.J. reluctantly agreed, and Teresa and Gus boarded the shuttle a few minutes later. They reached the room just in time. Gus threw up several times, then fell into a sound sleep for the rest of the day.

On the second day, because Gus was still quite sick, Teresa stayed with him while C.J., Leo and Drew spent the day at Disney World. That night Drew began vomiting and continued all through the night. Teresa, exhausted, had to call housekeeping in the middle of the night for fresh sheets.

Day three was no better. Teresa insisted on staying in the room with Drew, who was still very sick, and Gus, somewhat better, but still weak. C.J. took Leo to Disney World for the day.

Day four was a disaster! Drew was still vomiting when C.J. also began vomiting. Teresa spent that day on "bucket duty" for them both. When the two had finally recovered enough to rest, she took Gus and Leo to the pool. After swimming, the three walked to McDonald's for dinner.

On the fifth day Teresa was finally able to get to Disney World. She and Leo, who had remained resistant to the "bug," enjoyed every breathtaking second of the Soaring ride and several more rides before returning to the sick bay to check on their slowly recuperating family. That evening, even though several were still a bit shaky, the entire family took the shuttle to the Park to watch the fireworks.

On the sixth day, sadly, Teresa succumbed to the "crud," as the family now called the cursed bug. C.J. took the rest of the family to explore Downtown Disney while, not to be outdone by her predecessors, Teresa was violently ill.

On their final day, Teresa, weak, but ready for a change of scenery, joined the family for a trip to the Animal Kingdom. At last everyone was well enough to enjoy the outing! Exhausted, but still excited about the amazing experiences of the day, they arrived at their room.

"Now what?" said C.J. "This blasted room key isn't working. It must have run out of juice." He tried again, with no luck. "Wait here. I'll go get a new one," he said, and went down to the lobby.

As he approached the desk, the clerk looked surprised and angry. "Well, finally you're back! We've been trying to reach you. Surely you knew your checkout time was at ten a.m., sir. We waited for several hours, and then we had to move your things to the storage room so that we could clean the room in time for the new guests' arrival."

"What?" C.J. said. "You gave away our room? Obviously you've made a mistake. We have our room booked until tomorrow morning. Our flight isn't until tomorrow afternoon."

"No, sir, I'm afraid you're the one who's mistaken," the clerk said. "Your checkout time was this morning. I suggest you check your registration. Here!" He pushed a paper across the desk to C.J.

C.J. stared at it for a moment, then clutching the paper, he rushed back to the family to tell them the bad news.

Teresa stared at the paper. "No! No way! There's some terrible mistake! Call the travel agent right now, C.J."

C.J. phoned the travel agent, who assured him that the hotel clerk was correct. "Your checkout time was at ten a.m. Your package ended today, with your flight home this afternoon."

C.J. looked at Teresa and shook his head *no.*

"Here! Just let me talk," she said. C.J. handed her the phone. "I'm positive our flight isn't until tomorrow. Why wouldn't you have booked our room until tomorrow?"

His answer was polite, but curt. "No, ma'am. Your Disney World package ended with a flight home at 2:00 p.m. this afternoon."

"But . . . that . . . wasn't my understanding. We've obviously missed our flight. Now, how do you propose we get home?"

"Well, I'm sorry," he said, "but I suppose you'll have to book another flight."

By then Teresa was in tears.

After they retrieved their luggage, they checked with the airline. Since it was peak time at Disney World, they were unable to get a flight home until the next day. They bought five one-way tickets for the next afternoon. Fortunately, they were able to find another hotel room, considerably more expensive than their last room, for that night.

On the flight home they discussed their unforgettable vacation—the trip of their dreams! All agreed that Drew should win the prize for the most vomiting, and that Gus'

44

birthday was one that none of them would ever forget. Teresa and C.J. had spent most of the week tag-teaming various chores, being nursemaids for the sick, entertaining the "unsick" and shuttling to and from the Park.

They found some irony in the fact that, during their Disney World trip, most of the family had seen very little of Disney World, and Gus, the birthday boy, had seen practically nothing. Furthermore, this vacation turned out to be the most expensive vacation they had ever had—or, almost had! It truly was "Such a Deal!"

# On the Go

Ah, the countless joys of country life! My husband Fred's and my dream had been to move from the suburbs to a tranquil country setting. Finding a home on a small, wooded fishing lake more than fulfilled that dream.

Basking in the sun on warm days, herons and turtles perched lazily on logs as they watched us drift by in canoes or rowboats. At night the muted bass sounds of bullfrogs and the occasional hooting of owls lulled us to sleep. Deer and other wildlife wandered about, adding to our contentment.

The only drawback to our pastoral bliss was coping with an aging and unreliable septic system, which belched and threatened us for several years. Our problems were finally solved when we replaced the system, a move that lightened our tensions and our pocketbooks as well.

Day 1: Fast forward fifteen years to a Friday morning during the wettest June in years. Record rains had caused extensive flooding in our area. A random flush of our first floor toilet caused both the toilet and the nearby shower to overflow. What a mess! Immediately we called for help, leaving frantic messages with ROTO-ROOTER, several septic companies and plumbers. Apparently, it was an unusually busy Friday. We waited, and waited.

ROTO-ROOTER was the first agency to return our call. "Brian will be there in two hours," was all the secretary said.

What a relief!

The secretary made several calls postponing the service call before the final one. "I'm really sorry," she said. "With all this rain, we're being swamped. It's too late for Brian to get there today, but he'll be there first thing tomorrow."

*What a revolting development! Now what?* Afraid to run any water or flush the toilet, we dined out and spent as much time as possible away from home.

Day 2: As promised, early Saturday morning Brian appeared. *Help at last!* I had to restrain myself. I wanted to hug him! He checked the drainage system, then loosened the plug to the cleanout for the line to the septic tank.

He frowned. "This line should be empty, but it's full of water. Water's not going into the septic system—not good!" he said. "First, you should have that septic pumped out. If that doesn't clear it, I'll come back and rout out the drain pipe." He handed us his estimate for several hundred dollars, then left.

After another round of our frantic calls and messages, one septic company finally responded. Much later that day, a man appeared, pumped out the septic system and showed us a large root he had cleared in order to get the septic tank open.

"The system's fine," he said, "but the drain between the house and the septic appears to be blocked. It could be tree roots. If I were you, I'd call ROTO-ROOTER to ream out that pipe."

He handed us his bill for several hundred dollars and left. By now it was late afternoon. We hurriedly phoned ROTO-ROOTER and explained the problem.

The woman said, "I'm sorry! It's too late to get that work done today, but Brian will be out first thing on Monday."

So, that was that! We were forced to be creative, to find other alternatives for remaining socially acceptable, to meet our personal needs and avoid putting any water down the drain. We filled buckets with water, took sponge baths or, with our towels in hand, visited understanding neighbors for our showers. For more personal chores, we frequented fast food restaurants and businesses. Needless to say, we were "on the go!"

Day 3: Fred said, "All this running around is ridiculous! Why, back in my Boy Scout camping days, we just . . ." Raising his eyebrows, he nodded and pointed at the trees in the side yard.

"Oh, no! No way!" I said. "You can't do that! What would the neighbors think?"

"Aw, c'mon . . . they wouldn't even see me." He smiled. "Besides, you were a Girl Scout. Tell me the truth. Didn't you girls camp out and 'go' in the woods?"

"N-o-o-o! No, we did not! Obviously, Girl Scouts are more refined than Boy Scouts," I said.

He gave me a look which said, *Oh, sure you are! Sissies!*

I returned a look which said, *Eeeww! Gross!* I must admit I was rather pleased to have the last look!

But, as it turned out, Fred had the last laugh. He disappeared for a while, then returned. Looking victorious, he said, "I found the perfect place to go."

"Really? Where?"

"The Hilton Inn. It's close by and very clean, very nice. You just might want to go there, too."

"I can't believe you went to the Hilton to use their rest room. What if they'd stopped you and questioned you?" I said.

"Well, give me some credit," he said. "I thought of that. I took along my Hilton Honors card." He grinned.

My response was an eye roll. "Well, at least you didn't go in the yard! Just let me tell you the story of Pinky, my old school friend, a boy with carrot-red hair, a very fair complexion and freckles galore. While he was camping with the Boy Scouts, Pinky made a trek into the woods to do his 'chores.'

"He never lived down the words he shouted to his buddy: 'Hey, pass me a leaf, pal! There's no toilet paper out here!'

"Unfortunately, he had squatted in a patch of poison ivy. He developed a terrible itchy rash that made him so ill that he was hospitalized for a week. Furthermore, he never shook the nickname, 'Pass Me a Leaf Pal, Pinky!' "

Fred looked unimpressed.

Day 4: Early Monday morning Brian, now our new best buddy, arrived and reamed out the pipe.

"See this separation here in this pipe?" he said. "I recommend videoing the pipe to make sure there are no more breaks."

We agreed. Soon after, his supervisor Joel arrived and videoed the pipe. He shook his head. "Uh-oh! The pipe from your basement to the septic has two breaks, and the second one is huge. All your water's been running out into the ground and not to the septic."

Fred grinned. "No wonder the grass is greener on that side of the patio."

I groaned.

Joel smiled. "We'll need to dig down to the pipe and repair it, then put in a clean-out."

He called to arrange the work and gave us an estimate of several thousand dollars for the job. After I recovered from the shock, I thought about our challenges in the past few days, and I concluded that money is far less important than the luxury of indoor plumbing.

Day 5: The final work was begun early on Tuesday morning and was completed by noon. What a relief it was to return to normal life!

Finally, some good did come out of our trials. We now appreciate the simple conveniences we once took for granted, and we are again enjoying our blissful life in the country. Best of all, we are no longer "on the go!"

# The Perfect Ride

(In the interest of brevity, expletives have been omitted)

"Jim, John's on the phone. He wants to talk to you," said Penny.

"Hey, Dad, great news! I just found the best vehicle on line—a Jeep Cherokee. It's the perfect ride, exactly what I've been looking for, and the price is right. I can see it around 3:00 this afternoon. Can you drive me to Chicago to check it out?"

"Drive to Chicago? No! Sorry, John. I'd rather stay away from Chicago these days. Too much traffic—too dangerous! Why don't you call your brother? Brian knows his way around the city, and he knows lots more about cars than I do."

"Well, I was planning to call him and ask him to go, too, but I really wanted both of your opinions on it. But okay, Dad, I'll call Brian and ask him. Talk to you later."

"Bye, John." Jim could feel Penny's icy stare. "Yes, Penny, I know, I know . . . Don't give me that look. I feel guilty enough for not supporting John in this. He really doesn't ask for much . . . Okay, okay, I'll call him back and tell him I'll drive him to Chicago."

Penny smiled.

Several hours later Jim and his two sons were on the outskirts of Chicago.

Brian looked around. "Wow, this neighborhood looks pretty scary!"

"That's why I drove my truck today," Jim said. I wanted to drive a reliable vehicle in case we need a quick getaway."

"Oh, C'mon, Dad. It's not really that bad," John said, then paused. "Uh, never mind. I take it back. Check out that sign."

"HEROIN FREE ZONE," Jim said. "HEROIN FREE ZONE? Oh, yeah! That makes me feel much better about being here!"

All three laughed, though somewhat nervously.

Several blocks later, Brian pointed and said, "Oh, great! Look at that!"

A policeman was frisking six suspects who stood, arms raised and legs spread, against a fence.

"A fine neighborhood!" Jim said. "Just be on the lookout for flying bullets."

"Yeah, right! And I have more bad news, Dad," said Brian. "Your GPS isn't working, and I have no idea where we are."

Jim frowned. "Great! Just great! I knew we shouldn't have come here!"

"Calm down, calm down, you two!" John said. "Just give me a minute. I'll use my cell phone GPS." In a few moments he said, "Okay, you can relax now. We're almost there."

"Thank God for modern technology!" said Jim. "Still, you'd better be on the lookout for anything suspicious."

In a short while they arrived at their destination. All three checked out the Jeep, which seemed to be in good condition. John climbed in. It started hard, but the man assured him that, although it had a small quirk now and then, it would be fine. John drove it a few blocks, then turned around. All three men decided that, at the price, it was a good buy. Satisfied, he gave the man cash and finished the transaction. Then he climbed into his new perfect ride and drove away.

Jim said, "Okay, let's get the heck out of here before we get robbed, mugged, or worse! This place really gives me bad vibes!"

Brian said, "Okay, Dad, and you'd better hurry and follow John. He's the only one with a GPS. We don't want to get lost again."

"You're absolutely right!" Jim said, then stepped hard on the gas.

To everyone's relief, in an hour and a half both vehicles arrived safely at home without incident—the end to a perfect trip.

Guess again! Unfortunately, the perfect trip did not end here. Once the Jeep stopped, it would not start again. Of course, the ad for the jeep was no longer online, and there was no answer when John phoned the seller. Month after month, the jeep was in the shop, where the mechanics tried, without success, to discover the problem.

Fortunately, in time, John has learned how to overcome its quirks. When it has a difficult start, he runs it for approximately five minutes, then shuts it off. After a few minutes he starts it again, and it goes.

By tracking the VIN number, John has also learned that the Cherokee is a Katrina survivor. That fact may explain some of the Jeep's ongoing issues. When the temperature of the Jeep gets up to 200 degrees, John turns it off for a few minutes. When he turns it back on, it's good to go. He is still considering having the exhaust system checked out.

When asked why he did not try to return the Jeep when the problems first arose, John says that if he had not bought it from a questionable dealer located in a dark side street in Chicago, he might have done so. He prefers to avoid that neighborhood in the future. Furthermore, he considers himself and his family members fortunate to have survived the entire ordeal.

He says that the only part of the entire transaction that hasn't given him a problem was getting the title, although he admits that the title did give him a wicked paper cut.

When asked about the entire episode, Brian simply grins and shakes his head. He says he is trying to forget the wild trip to buy John's "perfect ride."

And finally, there is Jim, who has vowed that he will never, never go to Chicago again!

# No Strings Attached

As May, Carol and I walked into the grade school PTA meeting, Carol shook her head. "Oh, no! Here we go again! There can't be more than eight or nine people here, and some of them are teachers."

PTA meeting attendance had been steadily dwindling, except, of course, on potluck nights. Somehow, even those who rarely attended meetings rallied when food was involved. Our PTA motto had become: "If you feed them, they will come!"

Obviously, this was not a potluck night! We decided to spread out to make the audience appear a bit larger to the evening's speaker. May and I joined another parent in the front row and Carol sat with several others in the back row.

After a brief business meeting, the speaker, a young optometrist, walked haltingly to the front of the group. Looking uncomfortable, he shifted from one foot to the other and cleared his throat several times. He pulled out a handkerchief and wiped off his forehead.

May rolled her eyes at me, as if to say, "Poor guy!"

I nodded *yes*.

The young man's hands, which were shaking, clutched a bundle of very thick, white strings. He began to speak about the relationship of children's vision to the quality of their education, but our attention was drawn to his hands, which continued to shake as he twisted and untwisted the strings. His nervous demeanor made us uncomfortable, and we were relieved when he finally set the strings down next to his projector on the small table beside him.

Unfortunately, one fat string somehow caught on his fly and stubbornly continued to dangle there as he spoke. May poked me with her elbow. I stifled a giggle and looked down to hide my grin. Shifting restlessly in her seat, she was chuckling. I tried to concentrate on the speaker's words, but the string, at eye level, distracted me. Carol, sitting behind me, put her knee through the hole in the back of the folding chair and nudged me. Feeling giddy, I tried to control myself.

May elbowed me again and whispered, "How about that string?"

That was it! I snorted, then choked out a giggle. I could feel May shaking beside me and sniggering. Mercifully, the lights dimmed and the slide show began.

*This is terrible! Thank goodness it's dark. At least people can't see us now,* I thought.

May whispered, "I really have to get out of here. I just can't take it!" She slid out of her seat and disappeared.

Now I was undone. Shaking, I put my hands over my face and suppressed my laughter until tears trickled down my cheeks. I was trying so hard to be quiet that I was in pain.

By the time the lights came on after the presentation, I had managed to gain control. Walking to the speaker, I apologized for my laughter, saying that something had distracted me and set me off. He graciously smiled and said that he had not even noticed—a true gentleman!

As I approached the refreshment table, Mrs. White, my son Mike's fifth grade teacher, looking quite stern, said, "It's really hard to believe that some adults can behave more like children."

I said, "Oh, I'm so sorry . . . it's just that . . ."

She raised an eyebrow. "It was the string, wasn't it?" She started to laugh.

I shook my head *yes*, and soon we were laughing together, along with several others who had joined us. I cannot remember an evening when I have laughed so much.

Furthermore, that PTA meeting is one I will never forget. It would not have been the same with no strings attached!

## A Friendly Neighborhood

At last Tim and Lania were in the final stages of their two-year house renovation! In spite of its dilapidated condition and obvious years of neglect, the century-old house had charmed them at first glance, and they loved it even more as each glob of plaster, brush of paint and pounded nail enhanced its transformation.

But today was a different story. Early that hot summer morning George, the rather bossy carpenter they had hired to do the more skilled work, had bustled in and said, "Missy, you need to paint that big stack of boards lyin' in the garage. I need 'em first thing tomorrow. Just pull 'em into the front yard. Better get right on it!"

*Well, thanks a lot!* Lania thought. *That shoots the one day this week when I needed to do some other things. Of course, nothing I've planned could possibly be as important as painting those blasted boards!*

Then she reconsidered. *Okay, okay . . . it can't take that long, and, besides, how bad could painting a few boards be? At least we won't have to pay his exorbitant rate for this little bit of work!*

Sighing, she marched to the garage and began pulling out the long, heavy boards, one by one, then dragging them to the front yard. George, busy with another task, ignored her. The monstrous boards extended the entire length of the front yard, past the sidewalk and across the grassy strip next to the street.

Obviously, Lania had underestimated the job! An hour later, dripping with perspiration, she dragged along one of the last few boards. She glanced at George, oblivious to her misery as he lounged against the front step and sipped a cool bottle of water.

*Enjoying yourself, George? Taking a little break from the heat? You probably haven't noticed me here, schlepping these big boards to the front yard.* She shook her head. *Obviously, chivalry is dead!*

Swiping a wet lock of hair from her face, she took a drink from her water bottle. Even worse than the blistering heat were the withering glances from walkers and joggers as they high-stepped or tripped over the protruding boards. Some begrudgingly detoured around them and walked in the street.

George continued to relax, oblivious to the situation.

"Um . . . shouldn't we be putting these boards in a place where they won't be in people's way?" she said.

"Look around, Missy," George said. "No place left to put 'em. Too much construction stuff lyin' in the way. Just keep goin.' You've got them boards to paint, and time's a wastin'!"

"Well, George, I really think . . ." she began.

Just then a loud yowl and a hiss startled her, and she turned to see a man kicking at Thatcher, the family cat. *That's the last straw!* She marched toward him.

"You stop that! You leave my cat alone!" she shouted.

"Then call off your damn cat! He's attacking my dog!"

Thatcher, back up, hackles rising, was crouched, ready to pounce again on the small, fluffy black poodle cowering behind his master.

*Uh-oh!* she thought.

"No! Thatcher, no! Bad cat! You come here!" she shouted. Thatcher turned and scampered off down the block. "Uh . . . I'm so sorry, sir! Really, I'm very sorry!"

"Yeah, yeah!" he said, waving her away. "You need to tie up that vicious animal!" Still glaring at her and dragging the terrified dog behind him, he charged ahead and stumbled over a wet board. He cursed again. He staggered, trying to regain his balance, and inadvertently pulled the little dog, now toppled over on his side, across the wet boards, striping him with white paint. Finally, he stood upright, collecting himself, then turned and scowled at the sight of his multicolored dog.

"Oh, my! I do apologize . . ." Lania said.

"Well, that takes the cake! First, your cat attacks my dog and then you try to break my leg! As if that isn't bad enough, some crazy white-haired monster cat lurking around that corner attacked my poor dog right before your cat did!"

Lania was speechless. Their ferocious white cat Summit was running free outside. Although he was a good family cat, he had a history of viciously attacking dogs and even other cats in the neighborhood. She and Tim hated to get rid of him, but were at a loss trying to decide what to do with him. They had even discussed the possibility of putting him in pet therapy. There was no question—it was Summit who had attacked the man's little dog.

"Blasted cats! I really hate cats!" he grumbled as he stomped off with his trembling dog beside him.

Lania called to him. "Really, I am so sorry, really, really sorry!" He charged ahead without looking back.

*Oh, my goodness! What else can possibly happen?* She thought.

Miraculously, the day passed with no more serious incidents and only a few glares and sarcastic comments from passers-by who were inconvenienced by having to walk in the street.

Soaking in the warm tub that evening, Lania vowed to put the day's traumatic events out of her mind. As she began to relax, the unpleasant memories blurred together and were almost forgotten. She decided she should not dwell on them any longer, and she would not even trouble Tim with them. After all, he had his hands full with his job and the seemingly endless house projects.

On a sunny afternoon a week or so later, as she returned home from a walk, she saw Tim across the street chatting and laughing with their neighbor and a third man, whose back was turned.

"Honey, come here and meet John, our new neighbor. He and his family moved in a few weeks ago. I was just telling him what a great neighborhood we have and how friendly and compatible the people here are."

Walking toward them, she said, "Hello, John, I'm so happy to meet you. Welcome to our . . ."

Just then the stranger turned around to greet her.

". . . our neighborhood," she said.

She stood face to face with the irate jogger from the week before. His smile faded into a mask of stunned disbelief.

"Uh . . ." he managed to say, "I believe we've met before."

Lania swallowed. "Yes, yes . . . I think so." Her face felt like cardboard, burning cardboard, but she willed herself to smile. "And, welcome to our wonderful neighborhood. I'm sure you'll just love it here!"

# Thatcher

Thatcher, the extroverted tabby cat, was the "neighborhood" cat, though technically, he belonged to my son Tim, his wife Lania and their family. Thatcher was quirky and unpredictable. Unnoticed, he would follow neighbors inside their homes, then appear in their kitchens, bedrooms, cars, or wherever his feline spirit moved him to go.

One neighbor laughed as she related a typical Thatcher story. Hearing her poodle's frantic barking, she walked into the next room. To her surprise, there stood Thatcher. Barely giving her or her dog a glance, he stretched, then walked to her dog's bed and lay down for a nap.

Mattie, the family's white German Shepherd, often accompanied Lania on her walks. With Mattie's leash secured around one wrist, Lania would push the baby along in the stroller.

Thatcher, unless preoccupied with other mischief, would stalk them. Springing from behind a bush or tree, casting furtive glances here and there, he would run along behind them, then suddenly dart under a nearby parked car. Soon he would peek out, checking to make certain "the coast was clear," and slink back to the sidewalk and walk behind them again, only to dash under another parked car moments later. Neighbors who happened to be outside found Thatcher's antics quite entertaining.

When the addition to the family's home was under construction, the fearless tabby climbed the step ladder several times to observe the workmen, who were entertained and amused by the "crazy" cat.

There were, of course, exceptions. Nancy, one of Lania's fellow school carpool drivers, had an inordinate fear and, therefore, hatred of cats.

One day when Nancy had come to pick up the children, Lania, noticing that her daughter Ella's seatbelt was stuck, climbed into the back seat to fix it. Suddenly she heard Nancy's frantic scream.

"Get this cat off me! I . . . can't breathe . . . I-I'm hyp . . hyper . . . ventilating!"

Lania was horrified to see Thatcher proudly sitting on Nancy's lap.

"Get . . . it . . . off! Now!" Nancy screamed again as she waved her arms.

Lania leaped out of the car and into the front seat, grabbed the cat and tossed him out, to the ground. As she hopped into the back seat again to fix Ella's seat belt, she heard another desperate scream.

"Help! Help me! He's . . . back!"

Lania yelled. "No, no, Thatcher! Get out! Bad cat! Bad cat!"

Looking puzzled, the cat did not budge.  Lania bumped her head as she scrambled out of the back seat and rushed to the front again to shoo the cat out of the car. Once he jumped out, she quickly shut the car door. Both women were exhausted.

Nancy, still trying to catch her breath, said, "It's going to take . . . me a while . . . to get over this!"

The Google truck, which drives through and photographs every street in the United States, came to a sudden stop on Thatcher's block to avoid hitting the cat, napping peacefully in the road.

The driver honked. Thatcher did not move. The man honked again and yelled, several times, but the stubborn cat lay there, ignoring him.

Finally, the man grabbed his speaker and broadcast a ferocious "Meeeee-ow!" Thatcher, looking more annoyed than alarmed, stood up and leisurely walked away. However, to everyone's surprise, when the Google maps were released, the iconic and ubiquitous Thatcher appeared as a dot on that street.

Thatcher was the healthier of the family's two cats. A few years before, their older cat, Summit, had become ill and died. Now their old dog Mattie was failing rapidly, and Thatcher, too, was showing signs of aging. Then, one afternoon a large, vicious dog wandered into the neighborhood and brutally attacked and killed Thatcher. Of course, Lania and Tim, and especially the children, Ella, Abby and Nate, were heartbroken.

Word of his demise spread quickly, and the neighbors were saddened and angry. Janet, the neighbor across the street, received the news when she was at work. Immediately, she began to sob.

Hearing Janet crying, her boss was concerned. "Obviously, something terrible has happened to upset you, Janet. You should go home now. Take the rest of the day off. And, whatever it is, I'm so very sorry . . ."

Janet blubbered. "Oh, it's . . . it's . . . o . . . kay. Our neighbor's c-cat just died."

Of course, the neighborhood children were extremely upset over Thatcher's death. One child sent this sympathy note:

I AM SO SORRY
THAt ALL OF
YOUR Animals
died OR aRe
about to    I AM Sorry
die          if this
             gives you
                  bad
             memories

The children planned a memorial service, complete with refreshments, for their dear, departed cat, and all the neighbors were invited. The girls wore Hawaiian dresses for the celebration of his life, and all those who wished to share stories about him were invited to speak. The following poem was written in Thatcher's honor.

## Thatcher Cat

*He will miss our cool and beloved Thatcher,*
*He roamed the hood with the highest of stature.*
*Nine lives they say . . . Bah! He balked at that stat,*
*He was one lucky, toothless and beer loving cat!*
*Often found asleep in the street or out on a roam,*
*He perked up when Janet or Tonya came home,*
*But beware if for a minute you dare turned your head,*
*He'd be inside your house, even asleep in your bed!*

*Though sometimes confused as homeless—why*
*Would you think that?*
*About such a well-groomed house cat?*
*He was quite a socialite, traveling neighbor to neighbor,*
*He ate many dinners; tuna was his favorite flavor.*
*He had a peculiar meow and a low hanging belly,*
*He had quite an appetite for anything smelly!*
*It's sad when we think about that Chow who dunnit*
*Til you realize that Thatcher's now with his best pal Summit!*

Thatcher is gone now, but if, indeed, cats do have nine lives, we all hope that Thatcher is enjoying his second life. Certainly he will never be forgotten, and the stories of his escapades will bring smiles to his family and friends for many years. Rest in peace, dear Thatcher!

# A Monstrous Job

Reverend Macy and I, both board members of a local daycare center, were sitting at my dining room table and busily working on a revision of the organization's by-laws.

"Mommy! Mom-my! Got to go potty now! Now!" a little voice called out.

"Uh-oh! Coming, Mike! Please excuse me for a minute, Reverend. We're really making progress potty training Mike, and I don't want to keep him waiting."

The reverend smiled. "No problem. Go right ahead. I remember going through that stage with our children. By the time they tell you, it's urgent!"

"Right!" I said, as I dashed into the next room to help Mike remove his coveralls and training pants and get him situated on his little potty chair.

"What a big boy you are, honey! I'm so proud of you for telling Mommy you need to go!" I said, smiling.

He beamed. "I a big boy, Mommy!"

"Yes, you are! Call me when you're finished, and I'll help you get dressed. Then you can go back and play with your blocks."

"Okay, Mommy," he said as I left and headed back to the dining room.

Soon Reverend Macy and I became immersed in our project, and for a time, I forgot about Mike, who had been unusually quiet.

Suddenly he yelled, "Mommy! Mommy, Look!" as he ran into the dining room. "I a monster!" he shouted in a ferocious voice.

I gasped as Mike, stark-naked and grinning, ran into the room.

"I a monster, and I got a tail! See?" he said, pointing to his backside.

And we did see! Sections of toilet paper were streaming from his hands and from EVERY orifice of his little body. No one could have missed his "tail," which was impressively long.

"See, Mommy?" He grinned, pointing again.

"Oh, Michael!" I said, feeling my face getting quite warm. I hid my face in my hands and mumbled, "Oh, Reverend Macy, I . . . I'm so-o-o sorry!"

Shaking, doubled over with laughter, the reverend was unable to answer.

Recovering, I jumped up, ran to Mike and said, "Michael, come with me—right now!" I took his hand and marched him toward the bathroom.

Still enjoying his "moment," Mike marched proudly along beside me.

When I returned to the dining room, Rev. Macy was still grinning and wiping away his tears.

"Again, Reverend, I'm so . . ." I began ". . . so sorry and so embarrassed!"

"Don't apologize, please!" he said. "He's so little. And, don't forget, I have five children of my own. Believe me, I've seen it all! Honestly, I don't think I've had such a good laugh in a long while."

"Well," I said, smiling, "I guess it was pretty funny, at that."

"Oh, indeed it was!" he said. "A good change of pace. And, actually, we're almost done here."

"You're right. This job really hasn't been as difficult as I expected," I said.

"Now, I'd have to disagree there," he said, laughing. "In fact, I'd say it's been a MONSTROUS job!"

# The Bells Are Ringing

My husband Fred, an electrical engineer, who worked long hours, often brought his paperwork home in the evening, then stayed up late to finish it. When I asked him to do a household project, he would say, "Put it on the 'Honey-do' list. I'll get to it when I have time." Although his intentions were good, my "honey-didn't" list grew longer and longer.

Our manually operated garage door was unwieldy, a challenge for me as I struggled to open and close it. The ordeal was even worse in the hot summer and bitter cold winter. Eventually, we bought one of the first automatic garage door openers, a fairly expensive purchase for a young family, but a blessing to me.

The early models were made to be installed inside cars—a time consuming task. Fred intended to install the "clicker," as we called it. However, extremely busy with work, for months he had failed to do so.

He warned me, "This clicker was really expensive. Whatever you do, don't leave it inside the car because it could be stolen. Just carry it in your purse."

For a short time this arrangement worked. However, one day as I was leaving Sears, a loud alarm bell sounded. Instantly, a stern-looking woman rushed to me and grabbed my arm.

"What are you doing?" I said. "Let go of my arm!"

"Store Security, ma'am. Step back inside." The woman firmly guided me back through the door.

"I don't understand this," I said. "What's the problem?"

She gave me a threatening look. "Ma'am, just open your shopping bag. Save yourself some trouble."

"All . . . all right," I mumbled, as I noticed several onlookers staring at us. My face was starting to burn.

She opened the bag and checked the bill and the items inside. She frowned, looking disappointed. "Well, there's nothing wrong here. Now, remove your coat."

"What?" I said.

"Your coat. Just take it off."

I took off my coat and handed it to her.

She reached into the pockets, then turned the coat inside out. Looking disappointed, she sighed. "Nothing here, either. Now, for your purse. Open it."

*Good grief!* I thought. *I hate for her to see all the junk I toss into my bag.* Reluctantly, I opened it and handed it to her as I noticed a growing cluster of gawkers staring at us. I could feel my face starting to burn.

"Look," I said, "just tell me what the problem is."

"It's standard procedure when the store alarm goes off." She took my arm and walked me to a nearby counter, then turned my purse upside down. The contents poured out, some spilling onto the floor.

"My, you had a lot of . . . stuff . . . in there . . . and, uh-oh! Look here!" She held up the garage door opener. "I think I just found the culprit! Let's see." Clicker in hand, still holding my arm, she steered me outside through the doors. The store alarm sounded. She escorted me back inside, triggering it once more.

Looking disappointed, she released my arm and mumbled, "Sorry for troubling you. Your garage door opener set off the store alarm. You should take it out of your purse when you're shopping."

I nodded *yes,* then scooped up my belongings, shoved them back into my purse and left the store as quickly as possible.

70

When Fred came home from work that evening, I met him at the door and told him about my embarrassing experience.

He chuckled. "I'm sure it was just a fluke and it won't happen again. I'll get that clicker installed soon, but, in the meantime, remember not to leave it in the car. Someone will steal it."

I shook my head and walked away. *This is a no-win situation,* I thought.

When I was finally able to appreciate the humor of the incident, I told my friend Betty, who laughed out loud.

"I just wish I'd been there to see it," she said.

I laughed. "Oh, you would have enjoyed it, I'm sure, but the odd thing is that I've been in several other stores without setting off their alarms."

"It must be a Sears thing," Betty said. I agreed.

A few weeks later my friends, Betty, Judy, Joyce and I went shopping in Chicago. On the way, Betty insisted that I tell the girls about my Sears fiasco. They howled with laughter at my experience, and even I began to laugh about the incident. After lunch, as we walked through the entryway to Marshall Fields in Water Tower Place, a deafening alarm bell sounded. I froze, realizing that the clicker, still in my purse, must have set it off.

Seeing the security guard approach us, I dug into my purse, grabbed the opener and held it up. "I'm so sorry! This is my fault. My garage door opener set off the alarm. Here, take it and see for yourself." I could hear my friends sniggering.

Looking dubious, the guard took the opener and my arm, as well, then walked me out of the store. The alarm sounded, and then sounded again as we walked back inside.

He shook his head. "Okay, okay, I'm convinced, but I'd leave this opener in your car from now on, ma'am."

I looked at my friends and rolled my eyes. By then they were bent over, laughing hysterically.

Wiping away her tears, Betty said, "I'd never have believed how funny it was if I hadn't seen it for myself. It was . . . like a slapstick comedy. Just remind me not to go shopping with you until Fred gets that thing installed."

"You should've seen your face!" Joyce giggled. "Really, you need to get on Fred's case. Just put your foot down!"

Everyone agreed. Fred was in big trouble.

"Well, honestly," I said, "Fred is so busy at work, and he often comes home late . . ."

"No, oh no! It's that engineer thing—that one track mind thing," Betty said.

"C'mon! He's an engineer," Judy said, "and he can't get your electric door opener installed? It should be a breeze for him."

I nodded. On the way home we all laughed again about my embarrassing experience.

That evening I described the entire scenario to Fred and insisted that he install the clicker right away or hire someone to do it. Again he reassured me that he would do so as soon as he could. I tried to be optimistic.

The next few weeks were uneventful, and I had almost forgotten the recent fiascos. One afternoon as I walked into our local Carson Pirie Scott, a deafening alarm bell startled me. I froze. *Oh no! Here we go again!*

Immediately a formidable woman, obviously the security guard, rushed toward me and pointed her finger at me. "You—stop right there!" she said.

Just then I saw Joyce standing at a nearby counter. She looked at me in stunned disbelief, then laughed out loud and buried her head in her hands to stifle her laughter. I grinned, to the displeasure of the security guard. Now accustomed to the all-too-familiar routine, I smiled and offered my arm to her. Seeing no humor in the situation, she grasped my arm and marched me off to the side of the store.

Then came an instant replay of the now familiar scene, my showing the guard my door opener and explaining the situation, her walking me outside, then back into the store, twice setting off the alarm, and, finally, her reluctantly releasing me with the usual warning to avoid bringing the opener into the store.

Still giggling, Joyce managed to say, "I c-can't believe it h-happened again!"

Laughing uncontrollably, we staggered out of the store. I avoided looking back at the disgruntled security guard. Of course, that evening I described my latest trauma to Fred and insisted that he install the opener ASAP. He promised to install it that weekend. I waited. Again, nothing happened.

Several weeks later my daughter Beth was invited, at the last minute, to spend the weekend at her girlfriend's family cabin in Michigan. The girl's parents were picking up Beth right after school. Time was short. I finished packing her suitcase and took her spring jacket from the closet. Instantly, I realized it was too small, that she had outgrown it. I rushed off to Sears, the closest department store, and grabbed the first jacket that looked like her size. I paid for it and rushed toward the doors, but stopped abruptly as the alarm bell blared.

*Give me a break! I can't believe it's happened again!* I thought.

As the clerk yelled, "Wait!" the store security guard started toward me. I pulled the clicker from my purse. "Look! Remember me? My garage door opener set off the alarm last time I was here. Sorry! But, I really, really have to go now!" I turned and ran out of the store, leaving the two women speechless.

Beth and I arrived home at the same time. I pulled the jacket out of the bag. "Bets, here's your new jacket for the trip . . . and . . . oh, no!"

The security tag was still attached to the jacket. I realized I had dashed from the store before the clerk could remove it. I knew that pulling off the tag would make ink squirt out and ruin the jacket. My only option was to rush back to Sears and beg for mercy!

This time I left the clicker in the car. Going back into the store would be embarrassing enough without any added drama. Briskly walking in and ignoring the alarm bell, I rushed to the same clerk I had curtly dismissed minutes ago. Smiling meekly, I quietly asked her if she would please remove the security tag from the jacket as quickly as possible.

Giving me a cold look, she slowly, methodically removed the tag. Mumbling my thanks, then looking straight ahead, I rushed out of the store. I was certain that the security guard, having seen me grovel, was smirking with satisfaction.

That evening when Fred came home, I was waiting, ready for a showdown. Sparing no details in describing the latest incident, I demanded that he install the opener immediately. After a lengthy and heated negotiation which involved my threatening a moratorium on cooking, we agreed that he would so that weekend.

As promised, Fred did indeed honor our agreement, thus ending the saga of the garage door opener. I suspect that he finally got the job done because, through painful experience, he had come to believe that: "If mama ain't happy, ain't nobody happy!"

# Bike Blues

"Aw—not again! This really sucks! Someone stole my new bike! Unbelievable!" Brian cursed as he examined the severed rope cable in his hand.

Finally he had saved enough money and replaced his old bike, which, ironically, had also been stolen, with an expensive Scattante. He had spent the night at his buddy Jack's house and, upon leaving, discovered that his new bike, which he had parked outside, had been stolen.

"I can't believe it's happened again! There's no way I can get by without a bike. My car's on its last leg, and I can't afford to replace the bike right now. Besides, riding my bike clears my head after a day of teaching. Man, I need a bike PDQ!"

"Well, what're you gonna do?" Jack said.

"What can I do? Wait a minute . . . What would I do with the bike if I were the thief?" Brian smiled. "Of course! I'd sell it. Maybe the guy has a fence, or, just maybe . . . he'd put it on Craig's list. It sure won't hurt to look."

"Good idea," said Jack.

Brian logged on to Craig's List, and immediately smiled. There it was—a newly posted ad, including a picture, of a blue Scattante—his bike! *Perfect!* he thought.

Brian laughed. "Man, the guy who wrote this obviously doesn't know much about bikes, let alone grammar! Here, look at this picture. It's my bike. I'd know it anywhere."

He called the number listed, and a man answered. "Yeah . . . ?"

"I called about that blue Scattante bike in your ad. It looks good. Can I come see it?"

76

"Uh . . . dude . . . do you . . . have any . . . uh . . . weapons?"

"Wh-what?" Brian said. *What an idiot this guy is!* "No, no, of course I don't have any weapons. Why would I? Look, I just want to see the bike. I'm new here, and I need a bike to get around. That bike looks good."

Silence.

Brian turned and whispered to Jack, "I think he's high. He sounds weird!"

"Hello? Are you there?" Brian said.

". . . Yeah . . ." the man said.

"Can I see the bike this afternoon—to check it out?"

Another silence, then, "Uh . . . well . . . I guess so. Okay."

"Can we set up a time? How about I come see it in an hour?"

They set up the meeting for an hour later.

Brian said, "Jack, I'm so mad! I really want to beat up this guy!"

"No, man! Think about it! That won't get your bike back. Just call the cops."

Brian knew he was right, and he called the police.

"Are you sure it's your bike? How do you know?" said the policeman.

"I'm positive it's mine. There's no question. It was stolen last night, and the ad's newly posted with a colored picture of it. I took it to Moab recently, and I can see the red dirt. It's still on it."

"Okay. Give me the directions, and I'll meet you a block or two away, out of sight from the man's house."

They made arrangements and met a short time later.

"Where are the papers for the bike?" the policeman asked.

"Oh, sorry! I was in a hurry to get here. I didn't think about the papers. I'm sure I can find them."

"Well, without the papers, I can't go in and take the bike."

"We have to do something right away. I really need that bike back, and I have to get it before he sells it to someone else. If he has any sense, he'll get rid of it as soon as possible. Please help me."

"Okay, okay . . . go in and check it out. If you're sure it's yours, try to get it outside the apartment, away from the guy. Then call me."

Brian nodded, then walked around the corner to the house and knocked. A disheveled young man with a dazed expression opened the door and motioned for him to come in. Brian smiled. He was in the right place! His bike and four others were scattered around the cluttered, shabby room, and the cut locks were lying on the coffee table.

"Nice bike," Brian said. "Can I take it out for a spin?"

"Uh . . . no . . . I don't think . . ."

"Look, I can't decide on it until I ride it. Otherwise, there's no deal!"

The man glanced around nervously. "Well, I . . . guess it's . . . okay."

Brian walked the bike outside, and the man followed.

"Back off, buddy!" Brian said. "I need to ride it to see if I like it. Okay?"

The man looked confused, but finally he nodded and stepped back and stood in the open doorway.

Brian rode the bike around the corner, out of the man's sight, and called the policeman. "It's my bike. I'm positive."

"Look, I need the paperwork before I can give it to you," he said.

"Please! Just get the bike. I'll get the paperwork to you right away."

A moment later, lights flashing and siren blaring, the police car came screeching around the corner.

As soon as he saw the police car, the thief ran around to the back of the building. The policeman bolted out of his car and chased the man, who, by then, had disappeared into the maze of apartments.

The policeman returned a few minutes later, threw up his hands and swore. "He's gone!"

He called for backup. In no time two more police cars, brakes squealing, arrived, and several policemen spilled out of the cars and ran into the apartment complex.

Forty-five minutes later the police returned to the thief's apartment and, to their surprise, they saw a man running toward the door. He was stark naked, and giddy— clearly high. They caught him and cuffed him.

Grinning, the policeman brought the man to Brian. "Is this the guy?"

"Oh, yeah! That's the guy!" Brian said, stifling a laugh.

"So, tell me . . . why did you strip, buddy?" The policeman said.

Raising one eyebrow, the man smiled. "Hey . . . I'm no dummy, man! I was afraid . . . afraid you'd recognize me by my clothes, so . . . I just took 'em off!" He laughed.

"Real smart move," the policeman said, then winked at Brian. "There's never a dull moment!" he said, then cuffed the man and led him away.

A short time later, papers in hand, Brian reclaimed his new bike.

And these, my friends, are the bare facts!

## Pastoral Pleasures

Ann and her husband Bob planned a long summer's weekend—a relaxing drive through the Michigan countryside to see whatever sights they happened upon. The highlight of their trip was a stop at Alma, Michigan, to see Bob's Uncle Vane's much-celebrated oil well.

Parking at the outskirts of Alma, they followed Uncle Vane's directions. Ann was surprised to find herself approaching a cow pasture with a number of the large critters roaming about. She was puzzled to see a contraption which looked very much like a child's teeter-totter sitting in the center of a small grassy plot surrounded by a wire fence.

"Is someone afraid the cows will try to ride the teeter-totter?" she said.

"Of course not," Bob said. "By the way, that 'teeter-totter' is Uncle Vane's oil well. I can't believe you don't know what it is!"

"Well, it doesn't look like the oil wells in *Giant*."

"In giant? What giant?"

"You know . . . the movie with Elizabeth Taylor and James Dean. There were oil wells in it, and this contraption doesn't look anything like those oil wells."

Frowning, Bob shook his head.

"Oil well or not," she said, "I'm not at all sure I want to walk through the middle of those big ornery-looking beasts."

"We're perfectly safe to walk through them. They're just cows, and they're totally harmless. Besides, they're probably as afraid of you as you are of them. C'mon! Let's go."

"O-okay, Bob, if you say so, but please, let's hurry. Oh, no! Look! They're following us! They're much too close to suit me."

"Well, c'mon, then! Hurry!" he said. "This fence is low enough for us to cross over."

"Wait! Wait, Bob! I don't want to get stabbed by that barbed wire."

"Trust me, honey. I'm putting my foot on it to hold it down. Here, grab onto my arm."

Ann latched onto his arm and very carefully put her foot over the wire. To her surprise she climbed over the fence quite easily.

"Now, you hold the wire down with your foot while I get across," he said.

She set her foot on the wire as Bob swung one leg over the fence.

"Oww! Ow!" Ann screamed as she experienced the worst electrical shock imaginable. Immediately, she jerked her foot off the wire, which shot upward.

"Yeeow! #! *!" Bob yelled, obviously unprepared to be jolted in his "privates" with enough volts to knock out a large cow. "Put your #!*! foot back on the #!*! fence!"

"I can't! I can't!" she yelled. "You didn't tell me it was an electric fence!"

Glaring at her, he somehow managed to free himself, then hopped around yelling more deafening obscenities, which caused the cows to scatter in every direction. Of course, Ann was left to navigate back over the fence by herself.

The memories of that weekend have faded for Ann, though she is certain that Bob still remembers his jolting experience. Understandably, she has avoided bringing up the subject, saying something about letting sleeping dogs lie.

And the oil well? Well, Ann claims it wasn't much of an oil well after all. However, she does admit that she and Bob got quite a charge out of the entire adventure.

## More Anniedotes

### A Hearty Laugh
Collecting for the Heart Fund, Barb was going door-to-door in her neighborhood. She hesitated at one neighbor's door. The woman's husband had recently had a fatal heart attack. Would she upset her by asking for a donation to the fund? Should she leave, or should she stay and ask? The dilemma was making her quite nervous. Reminding herself that the Heart Fund was such a worthy cause, she took a deep breath and rang the doorbell.

"Hello," she said. I'm your neighbor, Barbara, and I'm collecting for the Fart Hund."

She gasped, as did the neighbor. After a moment, both of them began to giggle, and then they laughed. In fact, they laughed so hard that they had to sit on the front steps to recuperate.

Incidentally, Barb's neighbor did make a generous donation to the Heart Fund.

. . . . . . . . . .

### Timely
Willy was having coffee with his buddies and raving about his new hearing aids. "I have two new hearing aids. They're the same kind Ronald Reagan wears, and they're really good ones—very expensive."

His buddy Carl said, "Really? What kind are they, Willy?"

Willy looked at his watch, then said, "Oh, about 1:00 o'clock."

. . . . . . . . . .

83

## Keep It Clean

After my parents barely survived a head-on car collision caused by a drunken driver, I called my grandmother to tell her the alarming news and to assure her that my parents, though both seriously injured, were recuperating in the hospital.

"Oh, thank goodness they're alive!" she said, then paused. "I just hope your mother had on clean underwear!"

. . . . . . . . . .

## A Tasteful Comment

Dee was standing in a long line at her church buffet. As she moved along, she remembered that sometimes the dishes at these gatherings could be very bland.     In    a loud voice, she said, "Would someone please pass me the condoms?"

It took several minutes for the crowd's laughter to subside.

. . . . . . . . . .

## Blushing Birthday Girl

Ken, whose wife Vickii was a teacher, threw a surprise thirtieth wedding anniversary party at her school for her. He sent her thirty red roses and hired a barmaid/singer to come and sing a special song to her.

Though quite embarrassed, Vickii had to giggle as the woman sang, "Nobody Does It Better." The crowd was delighted. The Dean of Students liked it so much that he asked the singer to repeat the song.

. . . . . . . . . .

## Admiration

As Judy stepped out of the shower, her three-year-old daughter Stephanie walked into the bathroom. Stephanie's eyes widened as she stared at Judy's nude body. "What is it, Steph?" Judy said.

"Oh, Mom," Stephanie said, smiling, "I just love your feathers!"

. . . . . . . . . .

## A Rude Awakening

*This story took place over seventy-five years ago, when "rules of the road" were considerably more relaxed.

Uncle Harry, an M.D., was in the habit of driving to his brother's home several hours away and asking if one of the older children would like to drive his car on the two-hour trip on back roads to his medical meeting in Indianapolis. Once they arrived in Indy, he would treat his young driver to a delicious lunch at the lovely hotel where his meeting was held. Then his nephew or niece would spend a few hours exploring the fascinating hotel gift shops while he attended his meeting. Of course, the children were anxious to volunteer.

One day, when Uncle Harry arrived, only eleven-year-old Mary was at home. Harry decided that she was old enough to drive him and asked her if she would like to do so. Naturally, she was delighted. Her parents were dubious, but Uncle Harry convinced them that she would be just fine.

Once on the highway, Uncle Harry's routine was to relax and enjoy a little nap for an hour or so. Because Mary was driving so well, he soon relaxed and fell asleep.

An hour or more had passed when he awakened to hear Mary say, "Uncle Harry? Uncle Harry?"

Groggy, he managed to say, "Uh . . . yes . . . what is it?"

"If I wanted to stop this car, just how would I do it?" she said.

Immediately, he awakened and showed her the brake pedal. Then he asked her to slow down, pull over to the side of the road and stop. He decided to drive for the rest of the trip.

. . . . . . . . . .

### Grins and Giggles Galore!

Sometimes the simplest things have delightful results. When our grandson Sam was nearly five months old, although quite sweet, he was a very serious baby. Unusually observant for a little one, he constantly looked here and there, "taking it all in," and discovering the world around him.

One evening when I was babysitting, I tried various antics to get Sam to smile. Though not smiling, he seemed content sitting on the floor on his little blanket and watching his silly grandma perform.

I wondered what I could do next to entertain him. Then I noticed an empty carton of pop bottles nearby. Taking out a bottle, I put it on the floor and started to spin it. Sam's eyes widened, and his mouth flew open.

First, he smiled, then he giggled and next, to my surprise, he threw back his little head and began to laugh out loud. He laughed so hard—a real belly laugh—that I was afraid he would fall over. Chuckling, I spun the bottle again, and we both laughed until we were weak.

I still marvel that a baby that young could laugh so hard. That evening we enjoyed our silly little game several more times. I'm certain that, by the end of the night, we were both exhausted from all of our laughter.

Even now, when I recall little Sammy and me, sitting on the floor and laughing, I smile. This memory of our delightful time together is one I will always treasure.

. . . . . . . . . .

## Oops!

Margaret, who was at the doctor's office, was suffering from a serious illness, which was causing severe memory loss.

As she entered the examining room, the doctor smiled and extended his hand. "Please come in and sit down, Margaret. I'm Dr. Hanes."

After examining her, he said, "You're progressing well. When your lab results come in, we'll know even more. Then I'll be in touch with you."

Margaret stood. "Oh, thank you, Doctor . . ." *Oh, my, what's his name?* she thought . . . *Oh, I know . . .* Smiling, she said, "Thank you, Dr. Underpants!"

. . . . . . . . . . . . . . . . . . . . . . . . . . . . . . . . . . . . . . . . . . .

## Bridge Divas

My husband Fred and I were fairly new in the community. Lorrie, a friend I had met shortly after we moved to town, asked me if, by chance, I played bridge. I answered that I did.

"Oh, good! Then you must come and substitute in our luncheon/bridge club next Wednesday!" she said.

Excited at the prospect of meeting new friends, I accepted. On Wednesday Lorrie and I walked into a lovely home and the welcoming smiles of our hostess and the other ladies. The women, all considerably older than I, were gracious and friendly and quickly put me at ease.

Sitting down for lunch at a beautiful table set with linens and fine china, we all began to chat amiably.

Midway through the meal, Lorrie turned to me. Grinning, she said, "Oh, I almost forgot . . . Congratulations!"

"What?" I said. "What for?"

She winked at the others. "Ta da!" she chimed, spreading her arms in a gesture of presentation. "The girls voted you in! You're officially a member of this bridge club! Welcome!"

All the "girls" were beaming.

"Oh, my . . . well, uh . . . thank you," I said. "That's very nice of you . . ."

"And, lest I forget," Lorrie said, "You're the hostess next month."

I must have looked stunned. Quickly she added, "Oh, don't worry. There's nothing to it. The hostess prepares the table and the main dish, and her committee brings the dessert and side dishes. You'll see. It'll be a cinch!"

"Well then . . . all right. . . I'm . . . I'm sure I'll enjoy being in your group," I said, feeling anything but sure. I somehow managed to smile.

The day turned out to be very pleasant, with friendly conversation and lots of laughter and joking. The ladies were all excellent bridge players, actually bridge divas, and they were very gracious to me as they soundly trounced me in the game.

During the following weeks I stewed over my luncheon menu as well as my inferior bridge skills, but I worked hard to be ready for the big day. I reread "how-to" bridge books, polished silver, made certain the crystal and china gleamed and washed and ironed the linens. I slaved to make certain the house was squeaky clean. At last I was ready for the girls!

Bridge club day arrived. I gave the house a last look. The yellow daisies added a cheerful touch to the dining room table, which, I had to admit, looked lovely, and an inviting aroma wafted from the chicken casserole warming in the oven. I smiled. *Everything is perfect. What could possibly go wrong now?*

The committee arrived with their salads and dessert, and soon the rest of the members followed. After sitting and visiting for a short while, we walked into the dining room. When the girls "Ooed" and "Ahhed" at the sight of the table, I felt gratified. All the hard work had been worth this moment.

"So, whom did you get for a sub today?" Lorrie asked, nodding at the empty place at the table.

"What?" I said, noticing the empty seat for the first time.

"I was asking who your substitute is for today."

"Oh," I said, "I *was* the sub last month, and since I'm now a member, I didn't think I needed a sub." I could feel my stomach beginning to churn.

"Yes, dear," she said, "but we had two vacancies in the club, not one."

"Oh my!" I said. "No one told me we needed another sub. Goodness!"

There were audible gasps and stricken looks on their collective faces. I quickly added, "But I'm sure I can find someone to play."

Lorrie gave a short laugh. "Well, Missy, one thing I know for sure is that we can't play bridge with only seven people, so I really hope you can find someone."

"Just excuse me for a minute and let me make a few calls," I said.

I raced to the telephone and called several friends. No one answered. I left desperate messages on their answering machines, but I had a sinking feeling that no one would call back in time. *What on earth do I do now?* I thought.

My phone remained eerily silent as we continued lunch. I prayed, *Ring! Just ring!* Then my husband Fred walked in, greeted everyone, and walked into the den to use the computer.

Polly smiled. "Say, does he play bridge?"

"Why, yes. Yes, he does," I said, and immediately excused myself and followed him into the den.

"Fred, you have to help me!" I whispered. "I'm in a real bind here. No one told me I had to get a sub, and we're one person short to play bridge. I've called all kinds of people, and no one's answering, and . . ."

"No way," he interrupted. "I'm not playing bridge with a bunch of ladies."

"Really, Fred, I need you."

90

"No! Definitely no!" He shook his head decisively. I left to rejoin the girls.

"Well? Is he going to play?" Dora said.

I lied. "Um . . . well, he's . . . he's thinking it over." I couldn't devastate their hopes. *Surely someone will call, or Fred will relent—surely!*

However, lunch continued with no phone calls and no relenting.

"If you'll excuse me, I'll just get more rolls," I said, and immediately detoured to the den.

"Honey, no one has called me back. I desperately need you to play bridge."

Fred said, "Really, I don't want to play . . ." I gave him my most pathetic look. He sighed. ". . . but . . . I'll think about it. Now, I'm not saying I will. I'm only saying I'll think about it."

I rushed to the kitchen, grabbed the rolls and walked calmly into the dining room.

"Is he playing?" Lorrie asked.

"Oh yes, he's agreed to play," I said, smiling, and hating myself for my deception. I silently prayed for a miracle to get me out of this mess.

A bit later I excused myself to get the dessert, but, again, I headed straight back to the den.

"I can't wait any longer. I'm desperate! I'll make your favorites—Swiss steak, chocolate chip cookies, German chocolate cake—anything, anything and anytime you want—if you'll please, please play bridge today! I'm begging you!"

He sighed. His look said, "How could you do this to me?"

Then I made my last ditch effort. "You know I'd do it for you if you really needed me, don't you?"

That did it! He shook his head *yes*. "Oh, all right, all right! But it'll cost you," he grumbled as he shut off the computer. Then he paused. "So, what's for dessert?"

When he walked into the dining room, the girls were delighted, and I was saved. It turned out to be a wonderful day. Fred played cards brilliantly, and he was absolutely charming, chatting and joking, causing frequent delighted squeals and giggles from the girls. Several of them said he was so much fun that he should join the group.

Fred never regretted playing cards with us that day. It was definitely a win-win situation for all. He saved the day for me, and he has gotten incredible mileage from that afternoon. Not only has he been able to brag that the girls asked him to join the club, but also he has devoured more than his fair share of Swiss steak, chocolate chip cookies and German chocolate cake.

# Pumps and Circumstances

What an exciting time for the family! Tim, our younger son, was graduating from high school. Unfortunately, Fred was out of the country on a business trip, and our older son Mike was at college taking final exams. Beth, our daughter who was several years younger than the boys, and I were on our way to attend the graduation ceremony.

We had "dressed" for the occasion. Beth had on her favorite outfit, and I wore a go-to-church dress and high heels. As we drove toward the high school, I became a bit teary. Our younger son was graduating, certainly an important landmark for him, but I was sad to think of his being gone for his first extended period of time away from home. It was difficult to see another of our babies "leaving the nest." Sniffling, I grabbed a tissue.

"Oh, Mom, please don't start again!" said Beth. "It's so embarrassing!"

She was at that age when children, and especially girls, are embarrassed by almost anything their parents do, or say.

I willed myself to regain control. *Get hold of yourself. Shape up! Don't embarrass the child!*

We entered the auditorium. "Oh, rats!" I said, seeing that the only seats left were in some of the highest bleachers. "Well, Beth, I guess it's up we go!"

And up we went. Though it was difficult navigating the slotted bleachers in my high heels, I pressed onward and definitely upward as the band began to play a march.

"Mom, hurry up! They're starting!" Beth said.

I nodded, moving faster, climbing higher. We spotted two seats several rows ahead of us and rushed toward them.

Just as we reached the seats, my heel got caught up in the bleacher, and I fell forward, desperately grabbing for anything to break my fall.

"Oh! Oh, my!" I gasped as I grabbed the lap of a man seated in the row right behind the two empty seats.

"No, Mom!" Beth said. "Oh, no-o-o!"

"Oh, dear! I'm so, so sorry! Please excuse me!" I said, as I awkwardly struggled to remove my hands from the man's lap while trying to disengage my shoe from the bleacher and regain my balance. The maneuver took several tries, and the man laughed harder with each of my clumsy attempts. I could feel my face burning.

"I'm really sorry!" I said. "Really sorry!"

"No problem! Drop in on me anytime, lady!" said the man, grinning and elbowing the man next to him. The two men were thoroughly enjoying my predicament.

"Sor-ry!" I mouthed to Beth as we finally sat down. "Really, honey . . ."

"Mom, I am so-o-o embarrassed!" Beth whispered as she glared at me. "How could you do that? I can't believe you!"

"Sorry!" I whispered again.

Just then a voice boomed out, "Please stand for the National Anthem."

We stood.

I began to sing, "Oooh, say can you see . . ."

Unfortunately, the soloist and I were the only two people who were singing. I stopped abruptly as Beth groaned and put her hands over her face. The woman in the row in front of us turned and stared at me, and I could hear the men behind me chuckling. I dared not turn around.

Beth gave me an eye roll and an "if looks could kill" stare.

I whispered. "Really—I'm so sorry, Beth!"

She shook her head, *no*, and waved me away as we sat back down.

To my relief, the rest of the ceremony progressed without incident, though Beth, looking extremely annoyed, avoided making eye contact with me. I was certain my daughter would gladly have moved if there had been an available seat.

Afterward, as we drove to a nearby pizza parlor, Beth relaxed a bit, and she described my embarrassing misadventures to Tim in excruciating detail. Tim, thoroughly entertained, laughed out loud, and even Beth began to smile.

"Okay, I guess the whole thing was sort of funny," she said, "but, Mom, you have to promise to behave at Tim's graduation party."

"I promise," I said, as Tim and I exchanged conspiratorial winks.

Incidentally, the graduation party was a great success. Furthermore, I do not recall embarrassing my daughter even once, although Beth may have a different recollection.

# A Warm Cozy Dinner

*Would this day never end?* Fred yawned. Today had seemed a week long. The turbulent pre-dawn flight to Maryland had caused him to scribble his notes, now nearly illegible, and the day-long business meeting had been stressful, to put it mildly. He looked out the hotel window at the hazy sunset and sighed, already dreading tomorrow and more endless posturing, politicking and negotiating. Yes, today's meeting had exhausted him, and tomorrow was certain to be another relentless tug-o'-war. There was no compromising with this stubborn crew!

He rummaged through the items in his carry-on. *Where is that aspirin bottle?* His headache had escalated into a real doozy. He found the bottle and gulped down two extra-strength aspirins and a swig of water before going down to meet his cronies in the lobby.

"Hey, Fred," Brad said, "several of us are going out—you know, to kick back a bit. God knows we've earned a night out after today's fiasco. Want to join us?"

"No, no. Thanks. You guys go on. I'm beat, and I have a killer headache. I'll just grab a bite here and turn in early."

"Aw, c'mon, buddy! A night out'll help you relax. You'll forget all about that headache."

"No, really, I'm not up to it, but thanks anyway."

"Have your way, big guy, but you'll be missing out on a good party. Okay, guys, let's get on with the par-tay!" Grinning, Brad waved goodbye as he and the crew headed toward the door.

*Oh, I bet I'll miss a good one, all right!* Fred thought. *Party on, boys! Tomorrow morning will come very early!*

Running up a large dinner and bar tab was standard procedure on these business trips, but it simply wasn't Fred's style. Besides, he wanted to be at his best tomorrow. What he needed was a quiet meal and a good night's rest.

He went back to his room, took one more aspirin, grabbed his *Wall Street Journal* and then headed to the dining room. He smiled as he entered the room. The flickering candles spilled their soft glow onto the round tables with their white tablecloths and napkins. *Ann would love this restaurant. It was elegant, subdued, quiet . . . definitely her kind of place.*

It was still early. There were no other diners in the room. *All the better! Now I can read my newspaper in peace!*

The cheerful hostess greeted him. "Good evening, sir. You can sit anywhere you like." She handed him a menu. "The waiter will be with you right away. Have a pleasant dinner."

"Thank you," he said, as he walked to a corner table, then settled into a comfortable chair and began to scan the menu.

Soon the waiter appeared and took his order.

Fred unfolded his newspaper and began to read. *What a great idea to stay here for a quiet dinner!* He was already beginning to relax, and his headache was subsiding. He sighed. He could certainly use more light for his reading. When the waiter came back, he would ask him to turn up the lights a bit.

Immediately, he was totally absorbed in a fascinating article about the financial turnaround of a small company. This would be a great article to share with his boss. He shifted in his seat as he continued reading. The room seemed a bit warm, even stuffy. Yes, this article was right on the money!

He wished he'd brought down his notebook to jot down some of the key points.

The room seemed a little brighter now, and he could read more easily. *Good!* he thought. *Someone has turned up the lights. Apparently they've also turned up the heat.* He would ask the waiter to turn down the thermostat when he returned.

Whoosh! Fred jumped. "What the . . . ?" he gasped as flames burst through the center of his newspaper and quickly spread toward the edges.

"Oh, my God—the candle!" he yelled as he dropped the blazing newspaper on the table. He snatched up his napkin and fiercely beat out the biggest flame, then several smaller ones until the mess deteriorated into a smoldering, charred heap and a few glowing embers, threatening to reignite. He poured his glass of water on the embers, which sizzled.

Just then the waiter, tray in hand, appeared. He stopped, staring in disbelief at the dark, wet smoking heap of paper and ashes.

Fred opened his mouth to speak, but "Uh . . ." was all he managed to mumble before the waiter scurried from the room. He quickly returned with several pitchers of water and a large trash bag. He emptied the pitchers onto the embers until there was no longer any sign of fire, except for a smoky haze. Then he grabbed a napkin from an adjoining table and tried to fan away the smoke. He quickly folded in the sides of the cloth and scooped up the sodden mess, then dumped it into the trash bag and carried it out of the room. Not a word or a look had been exchanged between the two men.

When the waiter returned, Fred, embarrassed and still unable to speak, simply stared at him as he wiped and dried the table. Then, with a flourish, the waiter whisked a fresh cloth onto the table and left the room. In a few minutes he carried in a tray of napkins and silverware and reset the table exactly as before, this time, Fred noted, without the candle. Again, he left and quickly returned, carrying a steaming plate of food which he set down in front of Fred.

"Will there be anything else, sir?" he said.

"No . . . no. Thank you. This is just fine. And . . . I'm . . . I'm very sorry."

The waiter's face was unreadable. "No problem, sir. Enjoy your meal." Abruptly he turned and left the room.

Several other diners came into the room.

*Perfect timing!* Fred exhaled loudly. *Ah, yes,* he thought, *There's nothing like a warm, cozy dinner to relax a person!* Then he chuckled, a bit louder than he intended.

# The Christmas Surprise

My head was spinning. *Details! Last minute details!* The old Jello commercial kept playing in my head. *"Busy day, busy day! No time to make dessert!"* Re-lax . . . *one thing at a time* . . . I willed myself to take a deep breath.

"Mike and Tim, please pick up your rooms before you shovel the walks. Beth, after you vacuum the living room, could you please finish setting the table in the dining room? I have to leave in ten minutes to pick up Grandpa at the train station."

*Now, what have I forgotten?* I checked my list. *All done! Thank goodness!* Giving the house a final once-over was the last item. For several weeks I had been on a fast track with all the Christmas preparations—cooking, cleaning, shopping and running those unexpected last-minute errands.

Christmas without my mother, who had passed away a number of years before, was never quite the same for all of us, but especially for Dad. Lately he appeared to be slipping, mentally and physically, as if he had simply given up. I was desperately looking for ways to bring some joy and energy back into his life and, hopefully, to rejuvenate him.

My husband Fred had come up with a great idea. He had heard my stories of our family's watching the Andy Williams television show together each week and how much we loved his annual Christmas show. This year Andy Williams and his Christmas show were actually coming to a theater in our area. Fred suggested we surprise Dad by taking him and the children to see the show. Hopefully, seeing Andy Williams in person singing the traditional Christmas songs would help bring back Dad's treasured memories and get him into the Christmas spirit.

Driving Dad back from the train station, I was so excited that I could hardly keep from telling him about our plans, but I restrained myself. After settling him into his room, I went to the kitchen to finish making dinner.

Soon after I began, Mike, our 12-year-old, walked in. "M-m-m, smells good, Mom," he said.

"Mike," I said, "I'm going to tell you something, but you can't tell Grandpa. It's a secret. Okay?"

"Sure! What, Mom?"

"We wanted to make this Christmas a special one for Gramp, actually, for all of us, and we were lucky enough to get tickets to the Andy Williams Christmas show at the Holiday Star Theater for tomorrow night. Isn't that exciting?"

Mike shrugged. "Uh, I guess so. Who's Andy Williams?"

"Why, he's a really good singer. You've seen him on TV before, but you were probably too young to remember him. When I was growing up and even when I was grown, seeing Andy Williams' Christmas show on TV was a holiday tradition for our family. Dad and I think Grandpa will be so thrilled to see him again, and especially in person. Sounds like fun, doesn't it?"

"Yeah . . . sure. But . . . do I have to go?"

"Yes, yes you do! Grandpa would be so disappointed if you didn't. And so would Dad and I."

"Okay, Mom . . . if you really want me to. You're sure he's really that good? I mean . . . does he sing stuff I know? Stuff like rock and roll?"

"Well, I'm sure he'll sing some Christmas songs you know."

"Oh, all right. I'll go . . . if I really have to," he mumbled, and off he went.

I knew Mike wasn't thrilled, but I smiled, knowing he'd change his mind.

That evening, after dinner, Tim, our nine-year-old, said, "Hey, Mom, dinner was s-o-o-o good! Did you see Grandpa? He had three helpings of that meat!"

I laughed. "Yes, it's his favorite—Swiss Steak. Grandma used to make it for him all the time. Say, Tim, can you keep a secret?"

"Yeah. Sure. I'm pretty good at it."

"Well, we're going to surprise Grandpa tomorrow night and take him and our family to a stage show—the Andy Williams Christmas show!"

He looked puzzled. "Who's Andy Williams? Is he a ball player or something?"

"You're way too young to remember him," I said, then launched into my litany of Andy Williams and our family traditions, including the Christmas show. I just know Grandpa will be thrilled to see the show again."

"Great! Um . . . do I have to go?"

"Well, it is a family night. We'd all be disappointed if you didn't go. I know you'll enjoy the show—with all the music and costumes."

Tim shrugged his shoulders. "Okay, Mom," he said and walked away.

*Strike two!*

Later, as I tucked Beth into bed, I tried again. "Beth, Dad and I have a wonderful surprise for Grandpa, but you must keep it a secret until tomorrow night. Years ago, Andy Williams, a great singer, had a yearly Christmas show with lots of beautiful music. Our family loved watching it on TV. He's bringing his show to our area, and we're all going and taking Grandpa to see it. Won't that be fun?"

"What kind of show? Will there be a play? People dancing? Puppets?" she said, looking hopeful.

"Probably not, just singing, mostly Christmas songs."

"Oh . . ." She looked disappointed, then brightened. "Can we go for ice cream after?" she said.

I smiled. "I think that would be fun."

"Good . . ." She yawned. "I guess it'll be okay then."

I kissed her goodnight and turned out the lights. I knew I'd struck out, more or less, but I refused to be discouraged. At least Dad would be thrilled by our surprise.

The next night, after we finished a delicious dinner at our favorite restaurant, my moment finally arrived.

"Dad, we have a great surprise for you. Believe it or not, we're going to see . . . the Andy Williams Christmas show!"

Dad stared at me for a long moment, then frowned and said, "Well, who the hell is Andy Williams?"

## A Lasting Impression

It was a beautiful spring day in Chicago. Ann and her three schoolmates of some fifty years before—Harriet, Helen and Rita, were having a wonderful reunion. After cheering on the White Sox to a victory, the "girls" were on their way to Table 52, a gourmet restaurant owned by Oprah's former chef.

They struggled to hold their own in the mob moving toward the subway. Feeling like cattle being jostled and herded into the train car, they miraculously found themselves inside and relatively unscathed.

As the doors began closing, people behind them, desperately pushing their way onto the train, shoved them forward, compressing them even more into the throng.

Suddenly Ann found herself face to face, and body to body, with a surprised young man who, in the crush, had been backed into the wall. Neither of them could move. A line from a song—"Back to back and belly to belly"—kept running through her mind. She tried not to grin. She and the young man were definitely nose to nose, chest to chest and belly to belly, giving new meaning to the term "up close and personal!" It was an awkward situation, indeed!

Harriet, who was crunched beside Ann, smiled wickedly, then gave her a nudge and a meaningful wink. Rita and Helen, crammed directly behind them, saw Ann's predicament and began to laugh.

Though trying to remain composed, Ann could not suppress a giggle, and immediately mouthed "Sorry!" to the young man, who, avoiding her eyes, stared straight ahead.

With every lurch of the train, she pressed even harder against her new closest friend, and each time she stammered, "Oh, I'm sorry. So sorry!"

*What is this guy thinking?* She wondered. *He won't even look at me. He's probably wishing that this old gal molded against him was about forty years younger. Well, he has something there! I wish I were, too!*

*My! He must be ver-r-y nervous,* Ann thought, as the stale odor from his armpits assaulted her nose. *Shame on me! I shouldn't be so critical,* she told herself. *After all, the pressure of our situation could certainly make him perspire. Okay, okay, so he's uncomfortable, but no more uncomfortable than I am! At least he could smile and reassure me . . .*

Another lurch. "Oh, I'm so-o-o sorry!" she said.

*My goodness, I've apologized a lot! I just can't be quiet. I wonder why he hasn't responded. At least he could say, "It's okay, ma'am." Maybe he doesn't speak English . . . or he might be too embarrassed to speak . . . or, he's just plain ignoring me and hoping I'll go away. Fat chance of that!*

Rita and Helen could not contain themselves. With every lurch of the train, they laughed harder. Ann could feel their shaking, and she could not help smiling. Harriet nudged her again. Ann glanced sideways at her friend, who, grinning wickedly, was thoroughly enjoying her predicament. That did it! Ann giggled, and then she laughed out loud. Still, her hostage remained expressionless, making her feel even giddier. Although she tried to remain somewhat dignified, she found it impossible to control herself.

Finally, the train slowed to a stop. When the doors opened and people began to spill out, Ann was at last able to take a step back. Seeing his chance, without even a glance at her, her captive bolted for the door and disappeared into the crowd.

Ann said, "What? He didn't even say, 'Goodbye.' How inconsiderate—after all we've been through together! And here I thought I'd made a lasting impression on him!"

That did it! The four friends could not stop laughing as they staggered toward the door. To this day the memory of the man on the train remains a highlight of their reunion.

## The Way the Cookies Crumbled
## She Nailed it!

*Tuesday? Already? Where on earth does the time go?*
Sue shook her head as she looked at the calendar, then at the pile of recipes and cooking ingredients strewn about her kitchen counter. She was extremely late starting her annual three-day cookie-baking marathon.

Every year she looked forward to baking, decorating and delivering gift tins of cookies—peanut butter, chocolate chip, butter cookies and her favorite, oatmeal raisin, to her neighbors and friends. This year she was not only short of time, but even worse, she needed to bake many more cookies than usual. As a board member of the League of Women Voters, she was expected to bring dozens of cookies to the League Christmas party on Saturday, which was only four days away.

As Sue picked up the first recipe, she stopped to admire her perfectly shaped rose-colored fingernails. She was happy she had taken the time to have these lovely fingernails applied at the salon. *Check that chore off my list! At least my hands will look good on Saturday! Enough time wasted! It's time to get cracking!*

The race was on! She plunged into her task, which involved measuring, chopping, sifting, blending, shaping, baking and decorating her cookies. Soon her familiar holiday ritual began to take on a comfortable rhythm, and she chuckled, realizing that she was actually humming Christmas carols as she worked. She inhaled deeply, enjoying the sweet holiday scent permeating her kitchen. Christmas was in the air!

She baked all that day and evening, and by noon the following day she was amazed to have reached the half-way mark. Elated, she surveyed the trays of assorted cookies covering the kitchen counter. As she picked up one festively decorated cookie to admire it, she paused, then shrieked. "Oh, no! No!" One of her beautiful new fingernails was missing!

She began a frantic search, first looking all over the kitchen, then racing upstairs to whip off her bedspread and check the sheets, and, finally, trying to retrace her every footstep in the past day and a half. At last, discouraged, exhausted, she collapsed into a chair. The fingernail was nowhere. *Where could it be? When did I lose it?*

Sue felt a chill. There was only one place she hadn't thought to look. *Oh, no, please . . . Not there!* She rushed back to the kitchen and looked at the trays of baked cookies and those still cooling on the racks. *My fingernail must be in one of my beautiful cookies!*

She paced. She stewed. Then she stopped. *I need to get hold of myself and approach this situation logically. I need to figure out what happens to a nail baked into a cookie. Would it melt and disappear into the cookie, or would it remain rigid, making it easier to find?*

There was one way to find out. She would remove another fingernail and bake it in a cookie. Sue grudgingly removed a second fingernail—her big thumb nail—which would, hopefully, be easy to find.

She made a new batch of cookies and inserted the nail into one cookie, carefully placing it by itself on the right front side of the cookie sheet. She slid the cookie sheet into the oven. As soon as the timer went off, she removed the cookies from the oven and put them on the racks to cool.

A few minutes later her son called to say he would be late getting home. *Late again? This is getting ridiculous!*

*This kid is making a career of pushing my buttons! He would be late on the one night I could use his help!*

Fuming, distracted, Sue hastily removed the cookies from the rack and shoved them in among the others spread out on the counter. *Calm down! Just calm down!* she thought, then stopped to pour herself a glass of water.

She turned back to the counter and gasped. *Oh, no! What have I done now? Where's that cookie with the nail in it?* She leaned in closely to examine the cookies. They all looked alike.

Now two nails were lost, and probably both of them were baked into her cookies. *But which cookies? An even bigger question—who would find them? Her friends, or, worse, one of the special guests at the League Christmas party? Maybe someone would choke, or even worse—break a tooth!* She could almost hear their screams as they bit into the hard fingernails.

Dizzy with the barrage of ominous thoughts assailing her, she sat down. She could see the headline on the front page of the Saturday morning newspaper: "Mayor hospitalized after choking on cookies made by Sue Klett for the League of Women Voters Annual Christmas Party!" Even worse, she envisioned herself in a striped jumpsuit behind bars! She shook her head. *Stop! This is nonsense!*

There was only one thing to do—one painful thing to do! Grumbling, she began her penance, crumbling cookie, after cookie, after cookie. Soon she found the deliberately placed thumb nail intact in her most recent batch of cookies. However, even after destroying the rest of the cookies, she failed to find the original nail. She was left with a feeling of utter despair as well as a wastebasket full of crumbs.

Exhausted, Sue sat down on the kitchen floor and put her face in her hands. After a few moments she straightened up. *Enough of this pity party! I am not a quitter!* She would make a plan—Plan B.

After making herself presentable by shaking off the array of crumbs and flour adorning her, she drove to a gourmet market. There she bought an impressive number of cheese balls and boxes of fancy crackers, certainly pleasing the owner of the market and, hopefully, satisfying the League of Women Voters and her circle of friends.

In case you are wondering what happened to that missing fingernail, you will be amused to know that, several weeks after the party, Sue found it in a box of raisins.

And that's the way the cookies crumbled!

## Fun in the Sun

"Race you to the hot tub!" Liz said as she sprinted ahead of Ann. It was a glorious day in sunny southwest Florida, where the two women were vacationing with their husbands. Liz, who had recently recuperated from a mastectomy, was more than ready for "fun in the sun."

"Hi, Ellen," Ann said. "Hi, Jay," she said to Ellen's husband, who was sleepily basking in the warm, soothing water of the hot tub.

"Uh-hello," he mumbled, barely opening his eyes, then closing them again.

"Hope we aren't disturbing you," said Liz. "Mind if we join you?"

"Of course not," said Ellen, smiling. "C'mon in. The water's great! I'm glad to see you gals. Jay's too tired keep me company," she said, nodding toward her husband, a quiet man, who was obviously enjoying his restful soak.

The two women eased into the warm water.

"Mmm . . . how luxurious!" Liz said. "Our husbands have no idea what they're missing, hitting those golf balls around the course in the hot sun when they could be here relaxing with us."

Ann sighed. "You're right. This is truly Paradise! So, girls, what'll we do this afternoon?"

"After we're waterlogged, we may want to run downtown. There are some nice shops there," said Ellen.

Liz said, "We haven't been downtown yet. I did hear about a nice little dress shop there, and . . . oh! Oh, my goodness!"

"No-o-o!" said Ann as she saw Liz's prosthesis pop out from the top of her bathing suit and plop into the bubbling water, where it bobbed and dipped with abandon.

"What the . . . ?" said Ellen.

111

The three women stared for a moment, and then they began to laugh. Startled, Jay opened his eyes, which were instantly drawn to the cavorting prosthesis. His mouth flew open, but he could not speak. All eyes were riveted on the escapee, which danced wildly, performing its unique, animated water show.

Liz grabbed at it, but missed. She tried again. "Whoops! That's my . . ." and then she doubled over with laughter. She tried to capture it again, without success.

"Quite . . . a frisky little . . . rascal, isn't it?" Ann choked out, sending Ellen and Liz into hysterics.

Jay continued to stare in disbelief as Liz finally grabbed the wayward prosthesis and stuffed it back into her bathing suit. Then, without a word, Jay stood, climbed out of the tub and quickly walked away.

His hurried exit set the women off again, and it took them several minutes to compose themselves and wipe away their tears. Just then their friend Don walked into the pool area and, seeing them, joined them in the hot tub.

"Hello, ladies," he said, then settled down into the bubbling water and closed his eyes.

Ann looked at Liz and grinned. She leaned over and whispered, "Do it again."

"What?" said Liz.

Ellen, nodded *yes* and mouthed, "Yes, do it again."

Suddenly understanding, Liz grinned and shook her head. "No, I can't," she whispered.

"Yes, you can. Do . . . it . . . please," Ann whispered, giggling.

Liz sat for a few seconds, then rolled her eyes and smiled wickedly. She tugged at her suit. Out flipped her prosthesis, which plopped onto the water and began its wild, frolicking dance once again.

Hearing the women's laughter, Don opened his eyes. He looked surprised, then simply stared. Suddenly understanding what was happening, he threw back his head and laughed out loud, sending the women into another bout of hysterics.

The tale of the bobbing "boob" has become a legend which brings laughter to all those who hear it.

# You've Got to Be Kidding!

It was a Saturday night in 1981. With no stars or even a sliver of moon peeking through the inky black sky, Fred, our three children, Mike, Tim, and Beth, and I were crowded into Fred's old work car on our way to the movies.

The small, no-frills Vega, having a stick shift, consumed far less gas than our insatiably thirsty station wagon. Always practical, my husband Fred saved money wherever possible, only to spend it later on some surprise for the family, a spontaneous vacation or some unnecessary but coveted item, such as a new bike for the kids or a nice gift for me.

Because we were running a bit late, Fred took a shortcut through the dimly lit, narrow streets of a small subdivision.

"Oh, nuts! This is a dead end! I must have turned the wrong way," he said. "No problem. . . I'll back up and turn around." He backed a few feet, then shifted into first gear. The car did not move.

"Now what?" He tried again, with no luck. "This is crazy! What the . . . ?"

"Just go, honey!" I said. "We're going to be late."

"That's the problem. I can't go! The car won't go forward."

He tried several more times, then threw up his hands. "This car won't budge! It's messed up for sure." He thought for a moment. "It must have been the flood! That #!*! flood!"

"Sh-h-h, Fred! The children . . ." I said.

But Fred had a point. Unpleasant memories of the previous month rushed back. Our family had piled into our station wagon and set off to attend a family reunion several hundred miles away. The day after we arrived we received

114

an urgent phone call from our neighbor. It was the beginning of a long nightmare.

"You need to come home! There's been a terrible storm—record-setting! The river's flooded our entire neighborhood! It's a disaster! Our streets and basements are full of over five feet of contaminated water, there's no power, and the National Guard was called in to prevent looting! Last night they were shooting at the rats that are coming out of the sewers! To be safe, you'd better wait 'til tomorrow and come in the daylight."

Of course, we rushed back toward home to assess the damage and salvage what we could. On the way, we spent a sleepless night at Fred's mother's home and left eight-year-old Beth and the dog with her for several days.

Arriving in town the next morning, we parked the station wagon a mile or so away from our neighborhood, and then Fred, the two boys and I waded through the chest-high flood water to our home to assess the damage. As we walked along, I prayed that the rats would not bite any of us. We arrived unharmed.

Once home, we were somewhat relieved that, although the water had destroyed everything—our furnace, washer and dryer, toys, etc., in our finished basement, our first floor had remained dry. We learned that some of our neighbors had first floor water damage.

We were grateful that, in the midst of the chaos, several thoughtful neighbors had floated Fred's Vega on boards out of our garage to a higher, dry area several blocks away. As soon as possible, Fred made his way to the Vega and, after many tries, was finally able to start it. Immediately, he drove it to a nearby auto shop, where it was checked over and, miraculously, pronounced fit to drive. For the past month he had driven it to and from work without incident, but now, here we were, sitting in his Vega, which was stuck in reverse!

"Well, whatever the problem is, we'd better get to a phone and call a tow truck," I said.

"No way! I'm not paying a tow truck to do what I can do myself. I'll drive the car home. You know I'm an excellent backer." He gave me a smug look.

"What?" I gave him what we call *the look*, a meaningful, *You've-got-to-be-kidding!* look. "Fred . . . seriously, you can't back this car across those busy streets in the dark. It's much too dangerous. You'll kill us all!"

"No, oh, no! Daddy, please don't kill us!" Beth cried out. She sobbed, then covered her eyes and put her head down. "P-please don't, Daddy!"

Fred turning to me, returned *the look*. Frowning, he mouthed, "Thanks," then said, "Now, Beth, just calm down. I can do this. Really, I can. I'll back the car home very carefully, and we'll be just fine. You all trust me, don't you?"

The boys cheered their hero on. "Sure, Dad! Yes, Dad!"

Beth, head down, mumbled a reluctant *yes*.

I shook my head and stared ahead.

Obviously Fred misunderstood my silence as assent. "Okay, honey, you watch the front, and you kids keep a lookout for passing cars on both sides. I'll turn around, look out the back window and steer it home. We're a team! This'll be a piece of cake! Let's go!"

And, go we did! I said a silent prayer as, all eyes riveted on assigned areas, we embarked on the harrowing backward drive in the dark, out of the quiet neighborhood, across two extremely busy streets and onto several side streets. Ignoring several honks, angry shouts and Beth's occasional whimpers, Fred slowly, and, I must admit, skillfully, maneuvered the car backward and homeward without incident.

Caught up in the adventure, the boys cheered on their hero. Mike said, "Wow, Dad! Great job!"

Tim chimed in. "Dad, this is sooo cool! It's just like the Blues Brothers!"

Beth sniffled and covered her eyes.

"Aw, quit being such a baby, Beth!" Mike said. "This is really fun!"

"Yeah, Beth!" Tim said. "This is really fun!"

I sat in stony silence, except when I shouted, "Lookout! Slow down!" or, "Watch the right! Oh-oh! Car on the left!"

Certain that someone would report us to the police and that flashing lights would soon surround us, I said a silent prayer for our safety. To my relief, our bizarre backward drive proceeded without any trouble.

At last we made it home! As we backed into our driveway, I sighed, thankful that the ordeal was over and we were safe. For the rest of the evening, Fred and I chose to avoid any discussion of our adventure, or, for that matter, any discussion at all. At times, "Let sleeping dogs lie" can be sound advice.

By morning, the sun was shining, and the tension had dissipated—that is, until Fred made a surprising announcement. "Well, it's time for me to drive the car to the auto store."

"Drive it—backward? Really, Fred? Seriously? You're going to risk driving this car backward again, and in broad daylight? You've got to be kidding!"

"Well, it's bound to be better than backing home in the dark, isn't it?" He grinned.

"Not funny! Not funny at all!" I said.

He made a face at me. "C'mon! Loosen up! It's a short trip, only a few miles straight down the road. I'm certainly not about to pay a tow truck to haul the car that short a distance."

"Well, I'll bet you the ticket and court fees will cost a lot more than a towing fee," I said.

Fred was undaunted. "It's all set. I've already called the manager and told him I'll park the car in the back with the keys under the front seat. Honey, you can drive the wagon ahead of me, then bring me home. Boys, you can ride shotgun this time. Beth, you can stay home or come with us. It's your choice."

"No-o-o! I'm not going!" Beth cried out.

Mike said, "Aw, come on, Beth . . . please? Don't be a crybaby! This'll be fun. It's an adventure. I bet most kids don't get to do anything like this!"

"You've certainly got that right!" I said.

Tim grinned. "Yeah, Mom, I bet none of our friends get to do anything like this."

*Ouch!* I thought. *I just shot myself in the foot!*

Mike said, "Dad did great in the dark. Think how much better he'll be in the daylight. It'll be a blast! What do you say, Beth?"

Fred said, "C'mon! We need to get going. Beth, are you in or out?"

"Well . . . okay," she said, "I'll go, but I'm going to close my eyes! And you guys better not make fun of me!"

The boys nodded. The deal was made. I stomped off to my car, and away we drove. I was certain someone would report us to the police, and I admit I was secretly hoping that they would. I could imagine the police arriving and giving Fred a ticket, or at least a stern warning, thus proving me right.

But, again, nothing happened, except that several irate drivers honked, and one gave Fred an obscene gesture, which certainly excited the children. Several drivers looked amused.

What a sight we must have made! One driver actually yelled out the window, "Attaboy! Go for it!"

As it turned out, Fred deserves some credit. He was right about the car. The clutch had, in fact, been damaged by the flood. For some unknown reason, the car had performed normally for a few weeks before malfunctioning.

And, driving backwards—certainly a difficult feat, Fred had made two successful trips, thus saving us the towing fee and thankfully avoiding any damage to us or anyone else. Surprisingly, we were never ticketed or arrested by the police. The only down side to our adventure was that I could never say, "See? I told you so!"

In time, the memories of our two grueling rides have become rather humorous, and, of course, our family has a great story to share!

Almost every time we tell it, someone says, "No way! You've got to be kidding!"

## What Goes Down

It was a sunny late afternoon in south Florida. Reluctantly, I packed up my beach bag and the page-turner that had intrigued me for several hours and left the beach to prepare for our potluck that evening. My husband Fred, our children and their spouses had left before dawn for a long anticipated guided fishing trip in the Gulf.

The word was that the fish had been biting, and we were all optimistic about their catching the main course for our dinner. Fred, who had been in a fishing slump all week, was certain that today his luck would change—that he would be the one to land the catch of the day. Of course, all of us were rooting for him.

When the bedraggled, but ecstatic crew returned several hours later, they announced that it had been a great day. Proudly depositing several large packages of fish on the counter, they headed off for showers and some well-earned rest.

Only our daughter Beth lagged behind, and with a conspiratorial grin, whispered, "Mom, I have the best story to tell you. You're gonna love it!"

"I'm all ears," I said.

"Well, we'd fished for several hours, and, wouldn't you know it—everyone but Dad had caught a fish."

"Oh, no! Poor Dad!" I said.

"Wait!" Beth said. "It gets better. Suddenly, he yelled, 'Oh, boy! I've got one, and he's a big one, too!'

"His line spun out really fast, and he began struggling to pull it back. That fish was seriously a whopper, Mom! Dad would lean forward, then reel in the line like crazy, then lean backward. It was like a tennis match—back and forth, back and forth like that . . . until it happened."

120

"It?" I said.

Beth rolled her eyes, then laughed. "Yes . . . it! Mom, you won't believe it. I'm not exaggerating. Dad was really straining to land that fish, and suddenly, his pants just fell down, clear down to his knees!"

"Oh, no!" I laughed. "What a shame! And the fish got away?"

"No- o-o! No way, Mom! Dad just looked down at his drawers for a moment, then went right on fighting that fish until he reeled it in. Reeling it in took a while, too. Mom, it was so-o-o-o funny! Watching him, we all totally lost it. Even the guide was hysterical. And we decided to name the fish 'The Drop Pants Fish.'"

"I can't believe it!" I said, and we laughed until our sides ached. When I was finally able to speak, I said, "Well, I guess I can believe it. This isn't the first time he's lost his pants."

"What?" Beth said.

"You know, your Dad has absolutely no hips, Beth, none at all. Honestly, men have all the luck, don't they? Men never have to say, 'Honey do these pants make my butt look too big?'"

Beth grinned, nodding her agreement.

"Well, Dad had been dieting and losing some weight. Anyway, being quite frugal and also a creature of habit, he tended to put on his same old faithful, baggy pants every day. Occasionally, they slid right off his hips—or, I should say, his 'no-hips?' Each time I saw it happen, being the dutiful wife, I felt compelled to warn him: I told him he was really lucky, that one day he was going to lose his pants in a public place, like the Jewel Store, and get arrested for indecent exposure!

"His response, depending upon his mood, was either a sheepish grin or a 'you're-not-the-boss-of-me' look. I usually retaliated by giving him my most stern 'teacher look.' He was so lucky that the worst never happened."

Still chuckling, Beth and I agreed that men certainly can be stubborn.

That evening everyone enjoyed the fish dinner, and even more, they enjoyed teasing Fred about his "drop-pants-fish."

Once vacation was over, life was back to normal—at least for a while. Fred decided to lose some more weight. He went on a serious diet and, at one point, he had lost a total of 55 pounds.

Not surprisingly, the drop-pants scenarios became even more frequent. I kept urging him to buy a smaller belt and pants, but he ignored me, saying it was too soon, that he still had more weight to lose. And, of course, each time his pants fell down, I repeated my warning about his embarrassing himself in a public place.

Sometimes he would play deaf. Other times he would smirk, then hold up his hand to stop me and say, in a falsetto voice, "Fred, you're so-o-o lucky! One of these days you're going to lose your pants in public and get arrested for indecent exposure!"

I would just shake my head.

One beautiful fall afternoon we decided to clean out our garage. As I started to lift a heavy box out into the driveway, Fred said, "Here, let me do that."

He picked up the box, carried it outside and set it down. And—no surprise—his pants fell down. However, this time they dropped all the way to his ankles, and, even worse, they somehow caught his undershorts and took them along, too, right down to his ankles! We're all familiar with the term *moon.* Well, this was the entire firmament—the sun, the moon and the stars!

All we could do was laugh! Fred was so weak from laughing that he had difficulty pulling up that tangled mess of clothes, and we laughed even harder. Suddenly, I had a terrible thought that the neighbors might be outside watching this X-rated scene. I looked all around, but luckily, there was no one in sight.

When we had somewhat recovered from our fits of laughter, I shook my finger at him and gave him a meaningful look. Immediately, he put up his hand and waved me off. Then he turned and walked into the house.

Later, without a word, he got into his car and drove away. In several hours he returned with a new belt and two new pairs of pants which were a size or two smaller.

I am delighted to report that "no-hips" Fred has had only a few close calls since then. However, we all know that life is unpredictable. Stay tuned!

# Even More Anniedotes

## Traditions

Tim called home and I answered.

"Hi, Mom," he said. "I have a story to tell you."

"Great!" I said.

"Remember how you used to cut out footprints from stacked newspapers and lay them out for us kids to find clues to where you'd hidden our birthday and Christmas gifts?"

"Yes, of course I do."

"Well, we've kept up the tradition, and our kids really love it," he said.

"I'm so glad they enjoy it. You certainly did when you were children."

"Right! So, we did it for Ella's birthday this year. It was really late when we cut out the footprints from a stack of newspapers, a bunch at a time. We were really tired and did a rush job," he said.

"Yes," I said, "we always waited until all of you were asleep, and sometimes it was very late when we began cutting out the footprints and laying them out."

"Well, of course, the next morning after Ella had found her gifts, we picked them all up. I thought you'd like to see one of the footprints," he said, "and I just e-mailed it to you."

"Okay, I'll go look," I said.

I logged onto my e-mail and saw this footprint. I laughed out loud!

. . . . . . . . . .

**Out of the Mouths . . .**

Uncle Harry, a dear old uncle, after a long illness, had passed away. My sister-in-law Elizabeth decided that it was time for her nine-year-old to experience a funeral. As Brent walked up to the casket with his mother and Aunt Betty, the widow, he stared into the casket.

*Oh, how sweet! He seems quite touched!* his mother thought.

"Oh . . . wow!" Brent said. "Look at him! You'd think he'd just sit up and say, 'Aargh!'" He clawed the air with his curved fingers.

Mortified, his mother gasped, but a moment later Aunt Betty laughed, and the two women ended up doubled over with uncontrollable laughter.

. . . . . . . . . .

## Say What?

The family, all but Becky, who was almost thirteen, was seated at the dinner table. Her brother Bart said, "What's keeping her, anyway? We're all starving!"

After her mother had called to her several times, Becky finally walked hesitatingly into the dining room.

Seeing Becky's red, swollen face and her sad expression, her mother said, "Oh, honey, what on earth is wrong?"

Wiping away tears, Becky pointed to her splotchy face. "My acne! I-I'm just so sick of l-looking at these pumples filled with piss all over my face!"

The entire family, and even Becky, exploded into hysterical laughter.

. . . . . . . . . .

## A Way with Words

Don Bollmeier told this story. A number of years ago his construction company erected a press booth at the Gateway race track in Granite City, Illinois. They had taken pictures, which he gave to his daughter Dee, who had recently graduated from college. He asked her to design a full page ad to go in the St. Louis *Construction News*. Everything went well. He did not bother to review it. He simply told Dee to run it.

Several months later he was discussing the ad with his number one son Brent, who immediately said he was not going to comment on it, other than the fact that he was quite surprised that his Mom had let it run. Don explained that neither she, nor he, had seen it.

Brent said, "Well, you'd better read it, Dad."

The ad read: "When You Want to Get It Up Fast, Call Bollmeier!" It received many favorable comments.

126

## Dental Flaws

Nancy, eight years old, was fighting with her six-year-old brother Ken, who was armed with a miniature bat, ball and fishing rod. Nancy, feeling vulnerable, reached for a chair to hold up as a shield.

"Don't you throw that chair at me!" Ken said, then hurled the fishing rod at Nancy. It hit her squarely in the mouth.

"O-o-oh!" Nancy cried out.

Unfortunately, the impact of the rod loosened four of Nancy's front teeth and left two hanging by the nerves. The dentist, who was able to push the teeth back up into her gums, told her that, sometimes, the teeth will reattach themselves. Happily, the maneuver was successful and Nancy's teeth attached to the gum and remained in place.

However, over the next fifteen years, Nancy experienced a number of dental procedures—root canals, caps, and the insertion of peg teeth, which are not particularly stable.

Some years later Nancy, who was on a field trip with her Abnormal Psychology class, was observing a group of Downs Syndrome students.

"Now, what will happen if you don't brush your teeth?" the teacher said.

A student raised his hand and answered, "Your teeth will fall out!"

At that instant, to her surprise and horror, Nancy's front tooth fell out! The group enjoyed a hearty laugh.

The final episode in the saga of Nancy's front teeth occurred a decade or so later. Just before she was to perform at the Renaissance Fair in northern Minnesota, another front tooth had to be pulled. Even worse, the hole left was still slightly bloody and quite visible on Fair Day. However, as we know, "The show must go on!"

To Nancy's amusement, she received several compliments on the realism of her get-up as an itinerant peasant musician. Only her husband knew that the "make-up" was nothing of the sort!

(Nancy and I hope that the reader can sink his or her teeth into this story!)

. . . . . . . . . .

### A Logical Explanation

Marie and her daughter Kitty have been our dear friends—and more like family, for many years. When our children were small, these two "angels" often volunteered to babysit for them. Their kindness was such a blessing!

One afternoon, when Kitty was in her teens, she was babysitting for Michael, then five years old, at their home while Marie was at work.

Sitting impatiently on a chair, Mike was fidgeting, barely enduring a "time out" for his naughty behavior. Suddenly, he hopped down from the chair, removed his shoe and hurled it across the room. It hit a lovely flower-filled antique vase, which crashed to the floor and sent water splashing onto the table beneath it as well as the living room carpeting.

Now Mike was in more trouble than before, and Kitty felt terrible about her mother's beloved vase. The two dreaded Marie's return that afternoon.

When Marie walked through the door, Kitty quickly explained that Mike had thrown his shoe, which had hit and broken Marie's prized vase. Marie was speechless.

Mike's big brown eyes were filled with tears, and his face was angelically innocent. He blubbered, "M-Marie, I'm sorry! I-I didn't mean to throw my shoe and h-hit your vase and break it! And, it wasn't even my fault!"

"It wasn't?" she said.

"No, it wasn't!" he said. "It was Kitty's fault! I meant to hit Kitty. I threw my shoe at Kitty, and she ducked, and so it hit the vase and broke it!"

Marie had to leave the room so that Mike could not see her chuckling.

. . . . . . . . . . . . . . . . . . . . . . . . . . . . . . . . . . . . . . . . . . . . .

## One More Blessing

Our entire family of fifteen people, as well as our daughter-in-law Tara's parents, Ginger and Tom, were celebrating Thanksgiving together at our home. To add to the excitement, our son Tim's family dog, Solo, an eighty pound Golden Retriever, and Honey, our five-month old puppy, romped with abandon together outside and inside, among all of us. It was a happy and chaotic day, indeed!

Dinner was over, the dishes had been done, and the adults were milling about the kitchen/family room area and were ready to relax. The grandchildren, having helped with the clean-up chores, were anxious to go back outside to enjoy the unseasonably warm and sunny late November day.

Just then Solo, spotting something of interest outside, bolted toward our sliding glass door. Crashing into it, he knocked it off the track, causing it to career outward and downward, toward the patio. A collective gasp and shouts of alarm accompanied its descent, and—at that moment, a Thanksgiving miracle happened.

Will, our teen-age grandson, already on the patio, stepped toward the door, and, with outstretched hands, stopped it in mid-air. There were murmurs of relief as he eased the door down to the patio floor, and then everyone began to clap and shout thanks and congratulations to Will, our uncontested hero of the day. We were all very proud of him.

One of our group wisely reminded us, and everyone agreed, that Will's quick-thinking and action, his saving the day by saving the door, was one more blessing for which we should all be thankful.

# Stranger Danger

Fountain Park Chautauqua, in Remington, Indiana, is a two-week summer "camp" for those staying in rustic cabins, campers, and tents and also for the numerous daily visitors to the park. Chautauqua offers religious services, fellowship, entertainment (two programs daily), crafts and various activities for all ages.

One afternoon our two younger granddaughters, Kate and Claire, then nine and ten years old, were playing Legos upstairs in the family cottage.

"Whew! It's really hot up here!" said Kate.

"You're right," said Claire. "Let's go downstairs and get something cold to drink."

The girls bounded down the stairs, but suddenly stopped.

Claire gasped, then whispered, "Stop, Kate! Look! There's a strange man sneaking around our front porch!"

Giggling nervously, hearts pounding, they tiptoed quickly back up the stairs and ducked under the blankets on one of the bunk beds. They waited . . . and waited . . . for what seemed like hours, but was, in reality, only a short time. Listening, they heard no movements downstairs.

"Do you think he's gone?" Kate whispered.

"No," said Claire. "We would've heard that squeaky screen door shutting. I just hope he's not creeping up here."

"Do you think he is?" whispered Kate. "Listen to see if the stairs are creaking. He could be a robber or kidnapper! Do you really think he'd hurt us? If he comes up here, he would probably find us right away under these blankets. Now I'm getting really scared!"

"Me, too!" said Claire. "This isn't such a great place to hide. Besides, it's awfully hot under here. Let's get out from under these blankets and sneak part way down the steps and check."

Kate said, "Okay, but I just hope he doesn't see us. We'd be in big trouble then!"

Claire nodded *yes*. "Don't talk. Just whisper. We really have to be careful. Remember Grandma's warning about 'Stranger Danger'?"

Kate nodded *yes*. "Wait!" she said. "My iPad's on the dresser. I'll grab it and text my dad. He can't be very far away. For sure he'll come and help us."

She texted, *Dad, there's a strange guy on our porch. We really need help! Now!!*

In a few moments Mike texted back,
*Calm down, honey. Just stay where you are and wait for Grandma. She's on her way to the cottage right now.*

"I hope she hurries. This is so-o-o scary!" Kate whispered. "I really hope the stranger doesn't hurt Grandma!"

In a few moments they heard the screen door open, then some muffled voices below.

"That's probably Grandma. I just hope she's okay. That stranger could still be out there." said Claire.

"Yeah, I know," Kate said. "Listen! That's weird! It almost sounds like someone's laughing."

They waited.

"Girls? Kate and Claire? Are you up there? Come down and say, 'Hello' to Dan."

"That sounds like Grandma," said Claire.

Kate nodded *yes*.

"Uh . . . okay," said Claire. The girls looked at each other, shrugged their shoulders and came slowly down the stairs. They were relieved to see Grandma walking toward them.

Kate whispered, "Grandma, we were really scared when we saw that stranger on the porch!"

"Stranger?" Grandma said, then laughed." Oh, girls, come with me and meet the stranger."

She took them out to meet the mysterious man on the porch.

Laughing, she said, "Kate and Claire, this is Dan. Really, girls, he's no stranger. He's an old family friend and he's the uncle of some of your best buddies here at Park. I'm just surprised you haven't met him before now."

Relieved, embarrassed, Claire and Kate were grinning and giggling as they met "the stranger" on the porch. Both he and Grandma thoroughly enjoyed hearing the girls describe their frightening experience.

The case of "Stranger Danger" is now officially over, but Kate and Claire still laugh and blush as family members recount the story of their embarrassing, but entertaining adventure.

# The Untolled Story

This story took place over 40 years ago.

Our Fountain Park Chautauqua family cottage sits "a stone's throw" away from the back of the tabernacle, the open-sided building where various types of programs and religious services are held. A large old bell, which is rung prior to each event, stands behind the tabernacle. Sitting on our screened-in porch, we have a ringside view of the activity at the back of the tabernacle.

At Park, as we call it, the teens were (and still are) constantly playing pranks, such as putting chairs on top of the Park buildings and "T P- ing" (toilet papering) various cottages. Bill, a teenage friend and frequent "ringleader" of the Park pranksters, and my nephew Brent devised a unique prank. One dark night the two boys removed the clapper from the tabernacle bell and replaced it with a fake one they had made of crumpled up paper glued and shaped into a small sticky ball, which they then covered with coffee grounds. Surprisingly, their clapper looked authentic.

Laughing, the two boys told Liz, my sister-in-law and me, about their prank. They could hardly wait until the next day when Dick, the bell ringer, a family friend, would come to ring the bell. Imagining his reaction, we all laughed. Their prank seemed harmless enough, and Liz and I promised to keep their secret.

The next afternoon Bill, Brent and a group of young people, including Liz's younger son Brad, our three children, our niece Diane and several other young people crowded onto our porch to witness the big event. Giggling, we crouched down on the floor or sat, bent over, on the couch to conceal ourselves behind the waist-high porch wall as we anxiously awaited Dick's arrival.

According to schedule, fifteen minutes before the program began, Dick came to ring the bell. He pulled the rope. There was silence. Looking puzzled, he stared at the bell for a moment. Then, he pulled the rope again. As before, nothing happened. Frowning, he tilted his head, obviously mystified.

By now, hands over our mouths, we were all giggling. This was better than a slapstick comedy!

Dick bent over to look inside the bell, and apparently, seeing nothing unusual, straightened up and pulled the rope again. Still hearing nothing, he bent farther over to peer inside the bell, and then, looking confused, he straightened up and shook his head.

Now we were nudging one another, shaking with laughter and covering our mouths to stifle the sound. Trying so hard to restrain ourselves was actually painful.

Each time Dick tried to ring the bell, then bent down to peer at it, we laughed harder. It is surprising that he did not hear us, but obviously he was puzzled, frustrated and distracted by the mysteriously silent bell.

Finally, looking perplexed, he walked away, undoubtedly to tell the announcer about the silent bell and to ask him to announce the beginning of the program.

Unable to restrain ourselves any longer, our group totally lost control, laughing so hard that some of us were crying. I stumbled into the cottage to get a box of tissues to wipe our tears. By the time we regained our composure, we were weak from laughter.

Note: It has been suggested that this story could certainly be considered for the "No-Bell" Prize!

# No Fleas, Please!

On a sunny fall day my niece Barb and her dear friend Evonne were driving to Barb's family cottage in Fountain Park for a "girls' weekend." Since the two-week Chautauqua was over, they knew the park would be quiet and peaceful.

The gals were looking forward to reading, walking and relaxing in the park's lovely, tranquil setting. They anticipated hearing nothing but the chirping of birds, the chattering of squirrels, the occasional rat-a-tat of a woodpecker and the relaxing songs of the crickets. They had brought along books and walking shoes for long treks around the park and on the peaceful country roads in the surrounding area.

As they drove through the gate, Barb sighed. "Here we are, in Paradise!" She glanced around. "What happened to the sun? Paradise looks a little gloomy right now, but I'm sure it'll get better."

Evonne said, "Sun or no sun, it looks like Paradise to me!" She smiled.

They parked in front of Barb's family cottage and walked up the steps. Barb unlocked the door and they walked into the kitchen.

"Ouch!" she said. "Something just bit me! Oh, my gosh! It just happened again! Ow!"

Evonne said, "Oh! Me, too! Ow! What is it?"

Barb looked around. "Good Lord! Look! They're fleas! Eeew! They're everywhere! They're jumping all over this place. We have to get out of here right now!"

The two women, stinging from numerous bites, bolted out the door and slammed it behind them.

"Let's get to the hardware store before it closes," said Barb, as they ran to the car. "Rats! Now it's starting to rain!"

Barb bought a number of anti-flea foggers and they returned to the park. She quickly shed her shorts and sandals and changed to jeans and tennis shoes before entering the cottage and setting off foggers on both floors.

"Where did those fleas come from?" Evonne said.

Barb said, "It had to have happened this summer during the two weeks of Chautauqua. In addition to John's and my dog Bernie, there were my brother Bill's three dogs, Lobo, Sadie and Buffy, my brother Bob's dog Tessa and Mom's dog Becca. I could speculate, but there's no use pointing fingers now. I have the keys to my Uncle Bob's cottage, a few doors away. We'll hole up there for three hours while the fog works. It's starting to storm, so let's hurry! Then we can go back and air out the cottage after the fleas are dead."

Luckily, the girls had some playing cards and Sea Breezes in the car, and they were able to pass the time with no trouble. In several hours they returned to the cottage to air out the noxious fog, and a while later they returned and wiped down every surface in the cottage.

For the rest of the weekend they were able to read, relax and even walk, when the rain had subsided. They did, indeed, have some peaceful girls' time—just not as much as they had hoped.

Sometime later, when Barb told me the story, we laughed about the entire fiasco. Shortly after that, I found a sign, which says, "No Fleas, Please!" It still hangs above Barb's family cottage door as a gentle reminder to Barb's dog-loving family.

# Frankie's Adventure
(Based on an experience that happened many years ago.)

Frankie was a "good boy," and his Mom and Dad were very proud of him. He picked up his room some of the time, did his chores most of the time, and made good grades—all of the time. Pretty impressive for an eight-year-old!

However, at times, being a "good boy" could be downright boring! Several of Frankie's best pals, Rob and Pete, liked to brag about their exciting adventures—ringing the neighbors' doorbells and then running away, making prank calls and skipping school. How he wished he could have an exciting adventure, too!

Something inside Frankie nagged at him to "cross the line," to do something daring, something he could brag about to the guys. Skipping school would probably be the most fun, and that's what he decided to do. He would have a really exciting day, doing just what he wanted to do.

*I need a plan,* he thought. *This Friday would be a great day to skip school. Fridays are catch-up days, and Miss Green is always so busy helping people with their work that she wouldn't even miss me. Besides, I'm all caught up, so why do I need to go to school on catch-up day, anyway?*

Frankie grinned, just thinking about his upcoming adventure. He could hardly wait until Friday. He didn't even stall when it was time for bed on Thursday night. He didn't ask for one more glass of water, and he didn't ask to go to the bathroom after bedtime, the way he usually did. But when he climbed into bed, just thinking about his big day made him so excited that he tossed and turned and hardly slept at all.

Friday morning came very, very early. Mom had to call several times to get Frankie out of bed. Dragging himself out of bed, he suddenly remembered that this was Friday— his big day! He looked at the clock.

*Uh-oh! I'd better hurry up! It's getting late!*

He brushed his teeth, washed his face, dressed quickly and rushed into the kitchen.

"My goodness, you really moved along once you got up," Mom said. "How about some pancakes for breakfast?"

"Not today, Mom," he said, regretting his words already. "Just some cereal. I'd better get going."

"You're right. You don't want to be late for school. But I'll have your hamburger ready when you get home at noon, so you'll have a good lunch."

*Oh, no! I love Mom's hamburgers, but, not today! Today's my day!*

"Um, Mom . . . could I just take my lunch today? I'd like to eat with the guys."

"What? I just can't believe you're not coming home for a hamburger. That's your favorite lunch."

He felt bad about lying to Mom, but it was necessary. "Well . . . the guys are playing ball at noon, and I don't want to miss the game."

*Mom looks disappointed,* he thought. *Now I really feel guilty!*

"Okay, then, if you're sure," Mom said, quickly packing his lunch. "Aren't you going to finish your cereal?"

"Mom, I'm really full, and I don't want to be late."

"All right, then. Better hurry along!" She handed Frankie his lunch box and walked him to the front door. "Have a good day, Frankie."

"I know I'll have a real good day, Mom!" Frankie said, grinning.

139

She waved "goodbye" and Frankie started down the street, then turned and looked back. Mom had gone inside.

*Good! Now, where can I hide 'til school starts?*

He turned the corner and walked around the neighbor's house, then ran back to the alley and into his family's garage—a perfect place to hide. He would sneak out after school had started. By then the neighbors would have driven to work and wouldn't see him.

Once inside, he looked at his watch. Perfect timing! School was ready to start, but not for him! He smiled. *Today I'm free to do whatever I want! "Free as a bird," Dad would say. But, I'd better wait a while before I leave the garage, just in case . . .*

And he waited . . . and waited. *I bet I've been here an hour!* He looked at his watch. *Well, anyway, I've been here over 30 minutes. It sure seemed like an hour! It should be safe to leave by now.*

Just then a car drove down the side street. He couldn't take the chance of being seen; he waited a while longer. Every time he was about to venture outside, another car came by. He looked at his watch again.

*Almost an hour's already gone by! I've gotta get out of here, but I have to be extra careful. If someone sees me and tells Mom and Dad, I'm in big trouble.*

He sat down and waited. Just then he saw a big, hairy black spider crawling toward his leg. "Yikes!" he said, then jerked his leg away and whispered, "Get away! Go!" The spider came closer. He clapped his hands, and, miraculously, the spider turned and crawled away toward the wood pile.

*Wow! That was scary! That might have been a poisonous spider, and if he'd bitten me, I could have died out here, all alone.* He looked around. *There could be more spiders in here. I better get outta here soon, before anything else happens.*

*But where should I go? The creek! That's always fun. I could go fishing today, but my fishing pole's in the basement. I could go wading in the creek or climbing trees, but Mom and Dad won't let me go there and do that alone. They say the water's so deep and it's too dangerous! Rats! I know . . . I'll go to the school playground. There's great climbing equipment there. No, that won't work. Someone would see me.*

He sat for a while, trying to think of more things he could do. *There's always the park, but everybody drives past the park. For sure I'd be spotted. Anyway, none of that stuff is any fun to do all alone.* He looked around. *Hanging out in this dark, scary garage is no fun, either!* He shivered.

*What now?* He sat down to think for a few minutes. Then he saw a line of ants walking single file across the garage floor. Each one was carrying something that looked like a crumb, maybe a cookie crumb. Fascinated by how such a little ant could haul such a large crumb, he watched them for a while, until he yawned. He was getting sleepy. He closed his eyes.

He jumped when he heard a noise. He looked at his watch; it was almost noon. He must have dozed off.

*Lunchtime—already? Well, I'm kinda hungry. I didn't have much breakfast this morning. Wonder what's in my lunch box . . .* He looked inside. *Mmmm . . . cookies! Mom's chocolate chip cookies . . . and a turkey sandwich. I'll eat lunch and think about what I'm gonna to do next.*

He sat down and ate his lunch, every bite of it. He brushed away the cookie crumbs from his mouth and looked around. He smiled. *Those ants will have more crumbs to carry off now.*

Just then a car drove through the alley beside the garage, and he darted behind Mom's car to hide. He sat there for a while after the car passed.

*Well, I could just go for a walk and find something to do, but where can I go? Everybody knows everybody in this town, and I could really get in trouble. I guess I could read a story in my reader, but it's pretty dark in here for reading, and most of those stories are boring, anyway. Besides, my stomach kinda hurts. I think I ate too much. If I just sit here a while, maybe I'll feel better.* He yawned. *I'm kinda tired. I didn't sleep much last night. Think I'll close my eyes, just for a minute or two . . .* Suddenly a loud noise made him jump. His heart was pounding. *What was that?*

He got up and peeked out the garage door. It was a lawn mower. Mr. Robbins, the next door neighbor, was cutting his grass. Strange! Every day he went to work really early, before Frankie left for school, and he got home around the time Frankie came home. Frankie looked at his watch again.

*2:30? How could it be so late? I must've fallen asleep again. School should be out now, and I should be walking home. I can't believe I've spent the whole day hiding in this dumb garage. This has been the very worst day of my whole life!*

Grumbling, he grabbed his books and lunch box and walked out to the sidewalk. A short while later, he walked through his front door and put down his books and lunch box, just as he did every school day.

"Well, hel-lo, Frankie," Mother said, more slowly than usual ". . . and . . . how was *your* day?"

*Mom said "your" in a funny way and she raised one of her eyebrows.     Does she know?*

"Uh . . . it was fine," he said.

142

Mom smiled, then said, "Anything new today?"

"N-no, not really."

*She knows! I know she knows! I just hope she doesn't tell Dad!*

"Well, I better get going on my homework," he said, then hurried to his room.

First, he picked up his things that were lying around. Then he did all of his homework, and he even did some of the next week's work.

Mom came into his room. "Nice job," she said. "Since you're done early, I have a few more chores for you to do."

He mumbled, "Okay, Mom."

When his older brother Bob came home from school, he saw Frankie working in the yard. "So, what're you doing, squirt? Trying to rack up brownie points?"

Indeed, Frankie was trying to do just that, in case Mom and Dad had found out what he'd been up to today. He wasn't taking any chances. As Mom liked to say, "Better safe than sorry!"

Frankie never found out whether his parents knew that he had skipped school that day. And, of course, he was never punished—not really. Instead, he punished himself in the next few weeks by working very hard on his homework and by doing extra chores around the house and in the yard, even before he was asked.

And Frankie never, ever skipped school again!

# In Stitches

It was Claire's senior year of high school, and she was having the best time of her life. She had always loved school, but, as the daughter of a teacher and, even worse, a truant officer, in her school, she had felt somewhat set apart from her classmates.

Thankfully, time had alleviated the situation, and she now had a small circle of friends. Best of all, she finally had a boyfriend, a boy who had just moved to town and had no preconception of Claire, or of her father. What fun she was having, hanging out with her new boyfriend and three other couples! There was always something to do—some new adventure. She was overjoyed. Life was good, indeed!

As long as Claire could remember, she had enjoyed doing various kinds of needlework, including sewing and crocheting. Her sister Sue was a whiz at sewing, breezing through her projects, which always turned out to be flawless. While her sister's clothes were expertly crafted and fashionable, Claire felt that her clothes, by comparison, looked homemade and stodgy, even amateurish. Oh, how she longed to have a talent like her sister's!

Naturally, she was ecstatic when she managed to crochet a bikini which fit perfectly and was, in her opinion, quite flattering. She could hardly wait for spring and warmer weather!

As soon as it was warm enough, Claire, her boyfriend and their group of friends went to a nearby lake to swim. Although not a swimmer, Claire thoroughly enjoyed wading and splashing around in the water. Besides, she realized that this was her chance to show off her first real sewing success, her new hand-crocheted bikini.

She dawdled until the rest were in the water, and then she slowly shed her beach robe. Standing straight, head held high, she strode into the lake. Conscious only of her friends' admiring looks, she waded deeper into the water than she intended. Turning around to get back to more shallow water, she saw their smiles of approval and smiled back. Now they were actually grinning. What an impression she was making!

"Oh, Claire! Oh, no, Claire!" one friend yelled, and then she chuckled and laughed out loud.

Now all of her friends, including her boyfriend, were laughing, and several were actually bent over, holding their sides with uncontrollable laughter.

*What's going on?* She wondered. Just then, she became aware of a gentle weight, a strange pulling down sensation. Looking down at her suit, she gasped, "Oh, m'gosh! Oh, no!"

Her lovely bikini was slowly sliding down her body and stretching, the spaces between the stitches becoming wider and wider apart. *How could she have known that crocheted stitches drooped and spread when they got wet?* Her lovely bikini now looked more like a soggy, expanding fish net than a bathing suit—a look that was beyond risqué, and actually shocking, in 1971!

She suddenly felt as if she were in the middle of a movie where the teenage girl had just humiliated herself beyond belief with all her friends looking on. She was disgraced! Her face was burning as she frantically spread her hands in a futile attempt to cover the suit's expanding top, bottom and back. Mortified, she raced out of the water and grabbed her towel. She blinked back tears and shivered as she wrapped the towel tightly around her.

*This is a disaster! Will I lose my boyfriend? My friends?* Claire wondered.

145

However, as she stood there, clutching her towel, she glanced at her friends, who looked anything but shocked. In fact, they were hysterical with laughter. What a ridiculous situation! It was truly unbelievable . . . and funny—actually funny! Suddenly, she found herself laughing with them, and they continued laughing, wiping away their tears, until they were exhausted.

Of course, her friends teased Claire endlessly about the incident. The memory of her expanding bikini, a time when she was definitely in stitches, has stayed with her—and probably with her friends, for over forty-five years!

# Ella and the Mosquito

It was a balmy evening in Florida, and the air was electric with excitement as we entered the elevator. We pushed button three and began our slow ascent to the penthouse. My husband Fred and I were on our way to a lavish party with our visitors—our son Tim, daughter-in-law Lania and two young granddaughters, Ella and Abby, both looking like miniature princesses who had just stepped out of a storybook.

Abby, nearly two years old, was wearing an elegant white eyelet party dress, and Ella, five going on thirteen, was a vision in pink silk. Her doll Camilla, also dressed in a delicate pink dress, was tucked under her arm. Ella's crowning touch was her red sequined pair of Wizard of Oz Dorothy shoes, which she had proudly shown to everyone she had seen that day.

Ella felt like the belle of the ball! She was going to a grown-up party! She could not stop smiling because she knew that this would be the most perfect evening of her life.

And a perfect evening it was, except for one small thing, a pesky mosquito buzzing hungrily around us. That year all of us had been constantly warned about the dangers of mosquitoes carrying the West Nile Virus, and we had kept ourselves enveloped in clouds of Deet-laced sprays. We sprayed ourselves before and after swimming, after baths, before bed—just about every time we thought that the repellant might have worn off.

However, tonight we were in a jubilant mood, and mosquitoes were the last things on our minds. No one even noticed that lone mosquito buzzing about—that is, no one except Ella.

She saw the mosquito veering directly toward her grandpa. Sensing the immediate danger, she shrieked, "Mosquito!" as she grabbed Camilla by the feet and swung the doll with all the strength she could muster right at the mosquito. A loud thunk resounded as Camilla's hard rubber head hit that mosquito dead-on. Simultaneously, a strangled cry escaped as my husband doubled over, grabbing his crotch, where the now squashed mosquito had landed a nanosecond before Ella's devastating blow.

Fred groaned, and I gasped. "Fred, are you all right?"

It was one of those *you-had-to-be-there* moments, like a scene from a slapstick comedy, and despite my empathy for Fred, I began to laugh. Fred glared at me and continued to groan. As hard as I tried, I could not stop laughing.

Tim was no help at all. He rolled his eyes, then quickly turned away, faking a cough to mask his laughter. Lania, too, clamped her hands over her mouth and abruptly turned away as her back began to shake. Seeing their reactions made me laugh even harder. Ella, heartbroken at the realization of what she had done to her beloved grandpa, began to sob.

Instinctively, trying to comfort her while choking back my giggles, I said, "Fred . . . tell Ella you're okay now— please, tell her you're all right."

Fred, still doubled over and groaning, looked at me in disbelief.

Determined, I forged ahead. "Fred, tell her, please."

Now Ella was wailing.

"Oh, Ella," I said, "It's okay now, really. Grandpa's fine. He knows you were only trying to help him—to keep the mosquito from biting him."

Fred gave me one of those if-looks-could-kill stares. Lania and Tim, only slightly recovered, were still unable to speak. The only sounds were Ella's sobs, and I put my arms around her to comfort her.

After only a few minutes, which seemed much longer, Fred was able to stand upright again and managed to croak out, "Ella . . . it's all right. Grandpa's . . . uh, fine now."

The rest of us, after wiping away the tears and somewhat composing ourselves, managed to cheer up Ella and offer our belated concerns to Fred, who was still less than cheerful. After a short time we all left the elevator—some of us walking more briskly than others—and joined the party.

# How Alarming!
(This story took place nearly forty years ago.)

Fred made numerous business trips to Japan during his career and often brought home souvenirs for our family. Finally, he splurged and bought something for himself—a very nice Seiko watch, which he wore constantly.

The watch performed well, except for one glitch—the alarm rang every night at nine o'clock. At first, I assumed he had set it to remind the children of bedtime on nights during the school year, but it rang not only during the week, but also on the weekends. Several times I reminded him to turn off the alarm on the weekends because the children were allowed to stay up later.

Still, he continued to let it ring every night at 9:00 p.m., whether we were out playing cards, at the kids' sporting events—anywhere. The ringing became an object of conversation, amusing to some of our friends, but rather annoying to me. When someone asked Fred why it rang at 9:00 p.m., he would only smile.

Finally, I said, "Why did you set that alarm to ring every night at 9:00? Sometimes it just isn't appropriate—for example, the other night at the movies. We were lucky it went off during a noisy scene, but it was still embarrassing. The people near us stared at us. What if we'd been at a play or a concert?"

Saying nothing, Fred smiled.

"Did something memorable happen at 9:00 p.m. when you were in Japan?" I said.

The picture of dancing Geishas came to my mind, but I dismissed it immediately. Such a thing was definitely not Fred's style.

Still, he said nothing. He simply grinned and shrugged.

Then came the incident that provoked my wrath and a stern ultimatum. One evening, at 9:00 p.m., during a student's performance at our daughter Beth's piano recital, the alarm went off. The piano teacher gave Fred a stormy look, several parents glared at us and I cringed, sinking lower in my seat, hoping to become invisible. Of course, Beth was embarrassed and upset.

That did it! I pointed at his watch, then mouthed, "Shut . . . it . . . off!"

I was too angry to look at him after that, for fear he was smiling again. I had reached my limit. Enough was enough!

On the way home, I said, "Fred, I cannot believe your alarm went off during the recital. It was rude and embarrassing."

"Yeah, Dad," Beth chimed in. "My teacher looked really mad!"

I said, "Just tell me why you insist on letting it go off every night at 9:00 p.m. Please, Fred!"

He smiled, nodded *yes,* then whispered, "Later."

Once home, I hurried the children off to bed. Finally, after months of wondering, I would learn the answer to the watch alarm mystery!

"Okay, Fred, just tell me why you set that alarm to go off every night at 9:00."

He smiled sheepishly. "I didn't," he said.

"What does that mean?"

"Well," he said, "it just goes off then."

I frowned. "Then why don't you just shut it off or reset it?"

"I can't do that," he said.

"Why not?"

"Well . . . I bought it in Japan. Just think about it. The directions are in Japanese!" he said, chuckling. "I don't speak or read Japanese."

"What? In Japanese?" I started to laugh. "Well, you have to do something!"

"Okay, I agree, but most places in the U.S. don't sell Seiko watches, and I don't know anyone around here who speaks Japanese," he said. "Since I came home from the trip I've been too busy at work, and I haven't had the time to research it. I need to find a dealer or someone to translate the directions. I guess I'll have to stop wearing it except when we're home at night—or, I'll have to get another watch. My old one is shot."

"What a crazy situation!" I said. "You really need to find someone who knows Japanese soon."

Fred spent some time researching, and, fortunately, he found a Seiko dealer in Chicago who was able to help. He went into the city on the weekend, and the man turned off the alarm.

At last the mystery was solved! Best of all, Fred was able to wear his new watch without fear of the alarm's going off at 9:00 p.m. every night. What a relief to us and an end to a truly alarming situation!

# The Gift

Sue was a wreck. Tonight was the night she was to meet Russ' parents. She and Russ had been dating now for several years, and she was certain that he was the one, the man for her.

While she was teaching school in Indianapolis, she had been smitten by Russ, a cute med student with a boyish smile and a killer personality. Now they were in love, and Sue had never been happier, except for one nagging worry. *Would his parents like her?* Oh, how she had dreaded this important, but inevitable trip to meet them!

When she admitted her fears to Russ, he laughed, then reassured her, saying, "Oh, you'll love my folks, and I know they'll be crazy about you. There's absolutely nothing to worry about."

*Oh, sure, nothing to worry about—nothing at all! Easy for him to say!* He'd breezed through his introduction to her family. Instantly, he had charmed her mother, and, even her dad, who had scrutinized every unsuspecting date she brought home, had pronounced him "a fine young man."

But now it was her turn to meet his family—his parents and aunts and uncles, and she knew she was in over her head. Why, this was worse than her first day of teaching! At least she'd had four years to prepare for that, and she'd been able to follow a lesson plan. But this was uncharted territory for Sue. No, it was much worse—this was Outward Bound!

Besides, it was her birthday weekend, and she had so hoped that Russ would have a romantic evening planned for the two of them. But, no such luck! He had never even mentioned her birthday, and she was certain that he had forgotten it.

Oh, well, she had more important concerns now. Both his parents were doctors—Dr. Betty and Dr. Joe, and the only time she had been around doctors was when she was sick. What would she talk about with these people?

"Well, Dr. Betty, tell me about your latest case. So, do I seem sick to you? Any new diseases I should worry about, Dr. Joe?"

Oh, this was insane! What was she thinking? She needed to think positive thoughts, and focus. *Focus on what?* Well, for starters, she would focus on what she would wear tonight. First impressions were important. *How about the little black dress? Russ loved it. No, forget it—too revealing. Not the red one either—too festive for a little family dinner. The plaid shirtwaist was flattering, very nice, really . . . for teaching, but not for dinner.*

Wasn't there anything in her closet that was right for tonight? There was no time to shop for something new, either. Russ was picking her up in an hour.

Resisting the urge to cry, she sat on the bed. *What now?* She could cancel. She could say she was sick. *No, that excuse would never do.* Besides, what if Russ insisted on staying home with her? *Really, it's too late to back out, and, definitely, it would be rude.* Even if she stayed home, she'd have to do this all over again in a few weeks.

*Think!* There must be something she could wear. There was the green dress she'd worn to church last week. It was fresh and perky, and Russ had liked it. It would be perfect with her little pearl earrings. *Oh, yes, the green dress will be . . . just what the doctor ordered!* She giggled. *No*

154

*pun intended, Dr. Betty and Dr. Joe. Oh, Lord, what have I gotten myself into?*

An hour later, she and Russ were on their way. With him at her side, her mood lightened considerably. She smiled. Of course, she wanted to meet his family, and she wondered how she could have gotten herself in such a stew. *After all, how tough could this be?*

Before she knew it, they had arrived at the house and were being greeted warmly by his smiling parents and relatives. Amidst the hugs and chatter, Sue began to relax. These were very nice people. After a few minutes, Dr. Betty invited the ladies to join her in the kitchen for some girl talk and a glass of wine while she worked on dinner.

Wanting to be helpful, Sue asked, "Do you have a job for me?"

Dr. Betty said, "Well, you can knead the dough."

*Knead the dough? Knead?* Sue gulped. She was definitely not a cook! Her mother, always the perfectionist, had never encouraged her to cook, for fear that her daughter would mess up her perfect kitchen. Then, miraculously, Sue recalled a movie scene with a woman who was kneading dough.

Smiling, she said, "I can do that." She washed her hands and dug in.

The wine was good, the conversation, relaxed. Surprisingly, she was enjoying herself. And then the phone rang. After a brief conversation, Dr. Betty announced that she had been called to the hospital to deliver a baby, but would be gone no longer than an hour or so.

"Say, could someone get started on dessert?"

155

Russ, who had wandered into the kitchen, spoke up. "Oh, Sue makes the best apple pie. I know she can handle it."

Sue froze as the memory of her recent deception zapped her like a lightning bolt. For months Russ had hounded her about fixing him dinner in her apartment, and she had put him off for as long as she could. Finally, she had asked a friend what to do.

"Just buy a Pyrex dish, take it to a bakery, and they'll bake a pie in it. Then get some frozen vegetables to steam, and follow the directions on the package. Buy some deli chicken, heat it up and then toss a little salad together. Really, Sue, he'll think you're Betty Crocker!"

And, he certainly had. The plan had worked, and dinner was perfect.

Delighted with the meal, he had asked, "Sue, did you really make this pie?"

She had smiled, and cleverly answered, "Well . . . not entirely. I didn't grow the apples."

But right now, everyone was looking at her. Clearly, she was toast! Before she could stop herself, tears spilled down her cheeks, and she blubbered, "I . . . I can't. I can't do it."

"Why, you can't expect this poor girl to whip up dessert in an unfamiliar kitchen, in the midst of strangers," said Russ's Aunt—instantly, Sue's favorite aunt. "Sue, honey, you just peel the apples, and let me make the pie."

Sue was saved! His aunt took charge, and under her direction, the women pulled together a delicious dinner. And, as promised, Dr. Betty sailed in just before it was time to sit down.

At the end of the meal, Russ's mother carried in a lovely birthday cake, and the family sang "Happy Birthday" to a stunned and rather embarrassed Sue. This occasion was a birthday party for her, complete with gifts. Russ had not forgotten after all, and she was touched.

Everyone had been so thoughtful, so generous to her. It was impossible not to feel welcome in the midst of this warm family. That night, she was content as she settled into bed in the cozy guest room. She marveled at the senseless agony she had inflicted on herself, and she vowed not to invent trouble for herself in the future.

The next morning, on her way to breakfast, she passed the master bedroom and noticed a lovely fragrance. Tiptoeing in, she saw some small scented guest soaps in a dish on the dresser. *What a perfect thank-you gift for Russ' parents!*

Early the next week, Sue drove to a large department store in Indianapolis and ordered a box of the same soap to be gift wrapped and sent to Betty. She smiled, pleased with her choice, and she was certain that Betty would be delighted.

Several weeks later, Sue was surprised that she had received no response from Betty. She thought it strange that such a gracious and well-mannered woman had not acknowledged her gift. Then she chided herself. *Stop worrying. After all, Betty's a busy doctor with an impossible schedule, trying to deliver all those babies.* Still, concerned that the gift had been lost, she resolved to check if she had heard nothing in a week.

At last, a letter from Betty arrived. Sue tore open the short note, which read:

*Dear Sue,*

*Thank you for sending me such an unusual and practical gift! Your thoughtfulness in sending the feminine hygiene deodorant spray kit is most appreciated.*

*Sincerely,*

*Betty*

For an instant, Sue could not breathe. *This is horrible!* She had sent Russ's mother . . . feminine hygiene deodorant spray! She was humiliated! No, she was ruined! How could she ever face these lovely people again?

*What could have happened?* Frantic, she rifled through her papers until she found the receipt for the soap. Clutching it in one hand, she grabbed her keys and bolted out the door to the car. Her panic turned to anger as she raced to the store. Once inside, she found the manager's office and burst through the door.

Her tearful eyes ablaze with anger, she waved Betty's note and the receipt at the startled man, saying, "H-Here! Read this! How on earth could you have done this?"

His eyes widened as he read the note. "Oh! Oh, my! Well . . . miss, I . . . I'm at a loss here, and I am so sorry! I will see that this is resolved immediately. I will give you a full refund and I will send a letter of apology to your friend. We will, of course, send her the soap you ordered at no cost to you," he added.

Still inconsolable, Sue drove home and immediately wrote her own apology to Betty. For some time, the memory of the terrible mix-up haunted her, but, finally, thankfully, the incident faded into the past.

Two years later, after Sue and Russ were married, they were having dinner with Russ' parents. Suddenly, Joe started to chuckle.

"What's so funny?" Betty asked.

His eyes dancing with mischief, he turned to Sue. "You know, Sue, we love you like a daughter. But, I have to admit, a few years ago, I did wonder what kind of a girl Russ had brought home, one who would send his mother a douche bag for a gift!"

There was an awkward, silent moment, then a snort, a chuckle, and a sudden contagious explosion of laughter, which soon had them all weak and doubled over, wiping away their tears. It is not surprising that the story of Sue's unique gift has become a family favorite.

# You Can't Be Too Careful These Days!
## (practically verbatim as written by Heidi Vardeman)

Exodus 16:2-4

*2. "The whole congregation of the Israelites complained against Moses and Aaron in the wilderness. 3. The Israelites said to them, 'If only we had died by the hand of the Lord in the land of Egypt, when we sat by the fleshpots and ate our fill of bread; for you have brought us out into this wilderness to kill this whole assembly with hunger.' "*

Several years ago, Heidi, a local Minister, decided to practice her sermon while she was walking her dog in the woods. An acting teacher had once taught her that a good way to learn one's lines is to record each line followed by a period of silence. Then, when the recording is playing, you can say the line out loud after the recorded line.

She decided to use this method. She started with the scripture lesson—the passage on which she was preaching. It was from the book of Exodus, the story of the Israelites complaining to Moses after he had led them out of Egypt and while they wandered in the wilderness.

She was on the trail with her MP3 player and ear plugs. She heard the line of scripture when the Israelites were complaining that they had no food to eat, and that they were dying of hunger in the wilderness. "If only we had died by the hand of the Lord in the land of Egypt!"

She listened to the phrase, then repeated it out loud, with great expression. After all, there was no one there to hear her. "If only we had died by the hand of the Lord in the land of Egypt!"

Then she heard the next line: "You have brought us into the wilderness to die."

She repeated that line quite loudly: "You have brought us into the wilderness to die!"

Just then, she saw another hiker coming down the trail. As he came closer, he saw her and heard her cry out, ". . . into this wilderness to die!"

Looking terrified, he turned around and ran away as quickly as he could. He had no clue that he had approached a minister learning her lines of scripture. He thought he had run into a mad woman shouting about killing and death in the woods!

# Merci Beaucoup!

Because of a family emergency, Christy Johnson, the French teacher at the local high school, would have to miss her class the next day. She wanted to make teaching her class as easy as possible for the substitute, who most likely would be unable to speak French. Also, she wanted to give her students some instruction, or at least some practice in understanding French. She smiled. She knew just what to do. She pulled out an old video from the shelf and left it for the sub to show the class. *Mission accomplished!*

Upon her return, she was surprised to find her class in a jovial, if not a giddy mood, and she had to quiet them several times. Apparently, she was not "in" on the joke.

*Oh, well, it's a Monday morning. Sometimes the kids have to "come down" from the weekend,* she thought.

Just then a rather stern voice came over the speaker. "Ms. Johnson, could you report to the Principal's office, immediately."

Hearing more giggles, she said, "Class! Class, settle down! I'm sure I'll only be gone for a few minutes, and I had better find you studying for the quiz you'll be taking on today's lesson when I get back."

The principal, looking quite serious, met her at the office door and motioned for her to come inside. She was amazed to find several department heads and the Assistant Principal, all with unreadable expressions, sitting around the conference table.

"Ms. Johnson, please sit down. He cleared his throat and gave her a stern look. I'm going to get right to it. I would assume you were unaware that the video you left to be shown to your French class in your absence was . . . well, pornographic," he said.

"Wh-what?" Christy said. "Pornographic? Oh, my! No! I-I am so . . ." She could feel her face blushing as she tried to hold back the tears. She grabbed a tissue from her pocket. " . . . so sorry," she managed to say.

He held up his palm. "Please, apologies and regrets are of no use now. It was necessary to notify all the students' parents, and so far there don't seem to be any repercussions. At least, so far . . ."

"And the kids . . . ?" she said.

"As for the students . . . well, who knows? Knowing kids, they probably enjoyed the whole experience, and they might have learned a few things, too. Nevertheless, Ms. Johnson, we felt we needed to call the matter to your attention to avoid such embarrassing occurrences in the future."

"Thank goodness nothing terrible has happened as a result!" she said, sniffling. "It was so careless of me! There was an emergency, and I was rushing to leave. I hadn't seen the movie in years, and I certainly didn't remember that it was—risque!"

"As I said, nothing has happened so far. As I've also said, apologies and excuses are useless now. Let's hope such carelessness won't be repeated. The less said about the entire matter and the sooner it's forgotten, the better. You may return to your class now," he said.

"Oh, thank you! Thank you! But please, I hope you all understand that I am extremely embarrassed and very sorry."

Expressionless, the Principal nodded as he stood to indicate that the meeting was over.

Christy tried to regain control as she left the office and returned to her class. No wonder the class was so animated that day! *But what could she do?* She knew it was better to let things settle down rather than stir up the kids with an apology or an explanation. The day seemed endless. She wanted to go home.

Fortunately, in time, the embarrassing matter was almost forgotten, though she imagined whispered conversations, knowing glances, winks and nudges behind her back. In spite of her feelings, she was determined to maintain her dignity. Standing straight, head held high, she taught her classes. In time, she was able to share the story with a few of her good friends, who laughed so hard that she, too, began to appreciate the humor of the incident. Nevertheless, she could hardly wait until the end of the school year.

The traditional end-of-the year awards ceremony was a much-anticipated celebration of outstanding students and teachers. She sat among teacher friends in the auditorium as the different awards were announced. Suddenly she heard her name being called.

"Ms. Christine Johnson, please come forward."

*An award was something I certainly hadn't expected this year!* She thought.

"Ms. Christine Johnson?"

She rose and walked to the stage.

Beaming, the Principal presented her with a certificate. "Mr. Johnson, I have the honor of presenting you with an award for the most creative and informative French class of the year," he said.

*Was she imagining it, or did she actually see him wink?* She could feel herself blush as she noticed the Assistant Principals grinning, and several looking down as they struggled to suppress their chuckles.

"Merci beaucoup!" she said, smiling back at them and enjoying a long-standing ovation as she walked back to her seat.